NEW MEXICO MILLENNIUM COLLECTION

A TWENTY-FIRST CENTURY CELEBRATION OF FINE ART IN NEW MEXICO

KATHRYNE FOWLER   NANCY N. STEM

NMMC
SANTA FE

THE NEW MEXICO MILLENNIUM COLLECTION II

Published by: The New Mexico Millennium Collection, LLC
            Post Office Box 863
            Tesuque, New Mexico 87574
            505.995.2202

Design: Nancy Stem
Production Editor/Writer: Suzanne Deats

Printed in Italy

ISBN 0-9679034-1-6
Library of Congress Catalog Card Number: 2001097085

FRONT COVER

SALLY ANDERSON
Lemon Drop
Mylar on wood
41 x 13 x 5"
Courtesy Anderson Contemporary Art

SETH ANDERSON
Slice of Marble
Mixed media on wood
60 x 60 x 3"
Courtesy Anderson Contemporary Art

BACK COVER

VALDEZ ABEYTA Y VALDEZ
Shadows
Colored pencil
39 x 51½"
Courtesy Anderson Contemporary Art

CONTENTS

FOREWORD

STYLE
5 EUROPE TO NEW MEXICO

INNOVATION
9 TAOS MODERNS

VISION
13 AGNES MARTIN

DIALOGUE
16 SITE SANTA FE   A BRIEF HISTORY

ESSENCE
20 BILL BARRETT

CLARITY
22 NEW MEXICO GLASS IN CONTEXT

PARADOX
26 FRITZ SCHOLDER

THE ARTISTS
29

INDEX
125

JANET LIPPINCOTT
Untitled
Oil on Canvas
72 x 48"
Courtesy
Karan Ruhlen Gallery

FOREWORD

Today's art world in Santa Fe, Taos, and elsewhere is a robust reflection of New Mexico's century-old position of national prominence. As the next millennium gets underway, its promises and challenges are mirrored in the art and ideas that continue to make New Mexico a magnet for creative spirits as well as serious collectors.

New Mexico Millennium Collection II presents a selective overview of the wide range of artistic endeavors from the past and the present. Some are destined for lasting fame; all are participating in the magic that is New Mexico art. We also present a series of essays by notable scholars and observers that will serve as a fine reference to a geographically isolated art world that has stood for over a hundred years at the crossroads of diverse American cultures and art history.

We would like to thank all the artists, galleries, and collectors who have generously contributed their works and objects for publication in this book. Readers will be pleased to know that they may add these pieces to their own collections in many cases, and that most of the artists are producing new and exciting works of art on an ongoing basis.

Many thanks also to Jan Adlmann, David Witt, Arden Reed, Maiya Keck, Alice Klement, Patricia Kaye, production editor/writer Suzanne Deats, and other writers and researchers for their invaluable contributions to the content of this book.

Kathryne Fowler
Nancy N. Stem

STYLE
EUROPE TO NEW MEXICO

Paris was the navel of the artistic universe in the 1890s, not merely distant but light years in every respect from the poky, dusty frontier villages of Santa Fe and Taos in the territory of New Mexico. Yet it was in turn-of-the-century Paris, a metropolis bursting at the seams with painters and sculptors, many of them towering figures in the history of modern art, that the seeds of the "art colony" Taos (and ultimately Santa Fe) were sown.

Every young American moved heaven and earth to get to Europe in the 1890s since the great European academies, both state-run and private, offered an ambitious American artist a rigorous (if truly academic and conservative) introduction to their craft in the very midst of the western artistic heritage, its museums, cathedrals and palaces.

An additional incentive for an American painter, sculptor or architect to make the challenging and certainly expensive move to Paris (or Munich or Düsseldorf) was, of course, to achieve that sine qua non, a European education which they might deploy when setting up their ateliers upon returning to the United States.

It was in pursuit of that lustrous veneer of a Parisian artistic education that three charter members of the legendary Taos Society of Artists became acqainted. In 1895, in the bustling student haunts around the École des Beaux Arts and the Académie Julian, the foremost schools of the day, the Ohio artist Joseph Sharp regaled his American comrades, New Yorker Bert Phillips and fellow Ohioan Ernest Blumenschein, with stories of the spectacular landscape of northern New Mexico and its undoubted charms for an aspiring artist in search of splendid motifs. Within three years, Phillips and Blumenschein had made it to Taos and succumbed, like Sharp, to its "enchantment."

That enchantment, which would increasingly lure countless artists and writers to northern New Mexico, was a compellingly exotic mixture of its colorful Hispanic and Native American cultures with their ancient artistic traditions and of the limitless, ethereal landscape in which they had long flourished. To this day, these elements are still powerfully attractive to visiting artists who may initially have been drawn here by New

Mexico's increasingly internationally-known art scene.

In the first half of the twentieth century, Taos and Santa Fe slowly developed their conjoint reputation as an "art colony" environment, i.e. a salubrious place, far from the clamor and stress of the city, where one's art could unfold in the bracing thin air of a near-magical high desert plateau. For many decades, the "colony" of Taos/Santa Fe was a well-kept secret, but by the end of the twentieth century that secret was to be shared by travelers from throughout the world.

In the teens and twenties, many artists looked to Taos (and increasingly to Santa Fe) either to work for a season or to settle permanently. These are the years when major artists and writers carried seductive stories of the "land of enchantment" back to the artistic centers of the east and even abroad. The roll call of these stellar visitors is impressive, among them the painters Robert Henri, John Sloan, Marsden Hartley, John Marin, Stuart Davis, Edward Hopper and, of course, Georgia O'Keeffe (who first visited in 1917 but would not establish residence in New Mexico until 1949).

Important writers, too, are intimately associated with the legend of Taos and Santa Fe – among them, most famously, Willa Cather. (Her novel, "Death Comes to the Archbishop," the key work of American fiction associated with New Mexico, was published in 1927.) D.H. Lawrence and his wife Frieda, guests of the arts patroness Mabel Dodge Luhan, likewise burnished the growing international renown of the area.

The first meeting of New Mexico's first "art colonists," the so-called Taos Society of Artists, was held in 1915, as was their first official group exhibition in Santa Fe. The charter members, all of whom are immensely collectable in the twenty-first century, were Oscar Berninghaus, Ernst Blumenschein, E. Irving Couse, W. Herbert Dunton, Bert Phillips and Joseph Sharp. What unifies the work of this first generation of New Mexico artists is the European Beaux Arts tradition (sometimes referred to as "Academic Romanticism") which was their common bond. They did not disband until 1927.

The Santa Fe artistic community first coalesced when, in 1921, a group of artists calling themselves

JOHN SLOAN (1871-1951)
Corral in the Canyon
Oil on canvas
20 x 16"
Courtesy Nedra Matteucci Galleries

the Cinco Pintores (Jozef G. Bakos, Fremont F. Ellis, Walter Mruk, Willard Nash and Will Shuster) held their first exhibition at the Museum of Fine Arts.

Later migrations to Santa Fe, in the 30s and 40s, during the period of New Mexico's sudden popularity as a tourist destination (fostered by the railroads and the famous Harvey Hotel chain) brought many American modernists – artists variously influenced by European early modernist, abstract experimentation – to Santa Fe, particularly lending the local art scene a new, vanguard edge. It was in the mid 30s that Georgia O'Keeffe spent her first full summer at Ghost Ranch, north of Abiquiu, and the artists Emil Bisttram and Raymond Jonson conceived of their "Transcendental Painting Group" of artists dedicated to abstraction. One surviving and important painter who numbered in that early group is Albuquerque's Florence Pierce, today one of New Mexico's foremost minimalist, vanguard artists.

By the time of World War II, it was quite clear that art in New Mexico was a feisty, yet mutually stimulating congeries of illustrative "Academic Romanticism" of the earliest artistic settlers in Taos and Santa Fe; the Spanish-Hispanic traditions of Mexico; the brilliant and timeless abstraction of Native American art and design; and the mulitifarious Modernism of the art world elsewhere in America and in Europe. Effectively, this heady cross-fertilizing tri-cultural heritage maintains to this day.

After the Second World War, the inexorable discovery of Santa Fe and Taos by tourists and the proliferation of artists and new art institutions which would contribute to the accelerated growth in sophistication of New Mexico's art world, is truly remarkable. Certain individuals, institutions and events punctuate this extraordinary quantum increase in Santa Fe's (and much less so, Taos') reputation as a national art center by the beginning of the twenty-first century.

Sculpture in New Mexico in recent years has received great impetus by a handful of institutions, all in Santa Fe. First on the scene in the early 70s, the Shidoni Foundry in Tesuque, under the direction of founder Tommy Hicks, quickly became the state's primary bronze-casting facility. Today Shidoni remains a very popular resource for sculptors of every stripe and from all over America.

The only comparable competitor, the Art Foundry begun by Dwight Hackett, has carved out a fine reputation among contemporary artists who, in addition to casting in bronze, seek to create unconventional works in newer media such as iron, wax, rubber and aluminium. Many major American artists have worked side by side with the foundry's master craftsmen.

Finally, the Sculpture Project at the College of Santa Fe, under the direction of Rick Fisher, annually mounts a very ambitious show of hundreds of pieces of contemporary sculpture scattered throughout the campus' buildings and grounds. For many artists, inclusion in that exhibition constitutes an important step in their careers.

For the advancement of Native American artists in New Mexico, the primary educational and advocacy institution is the Institute of American Indian Arts in

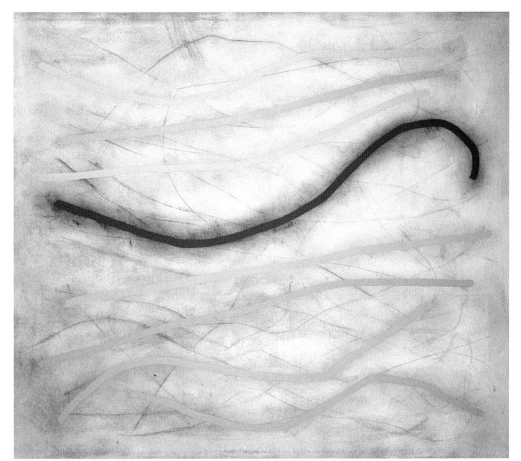

Santa Fe. Through the IAIA, such important Native artists as Fritz Scholder, T.C. Cannon and Darren Vigil Gray have reached national prominence. Santa Fe's Wheelwright Museum of the American Indian has also served to advance the reputations of many contemporary Indian painters, sculptors and craftspersons.

In Taos, the Harwood Foundation and Museum (administered by the University of New Mexico) and, in Santa Fe, the emerging artists' center "Plan B" are key institutions championing contemporary art.

Absolutely essential to the current worldwide reputation of Santa Fe as a significant art center was the founding of SITE Santa Fe. In 1995, galvanized by a handful of movers, shakers and the well-heeled, and spurred by the driving force of art dealer Laura Carpenter (no longer a Santa Fe art player), SITE debuted with its first Biennial of Contemporary Art with a theme drawn from a phrase of Georgia O'Keeffe describing New Mexico as her "faraway nearby." Four SITE biennials

later, the institution has evolved into a world-recognized *kunsthalle* and, simultaneously, a year-round community resource.

A parting word must be said – indeed, attention must be paid – regarding the role of a number of women instrumental in the presentation of cutting edge art and globally-savvy art in Santa Fe.

Linda Durham, through two decades, has shifted her location several times to acquire ever more ample exhibition space for her stable, which has always included a number of artists whose work absolutely demanded such expanse of display. That stable of artists grew to include a large and impressive number of non-objective New Mexico artists (though not exclusively non-objective), a number of whom have achieved substantial national reputations through Durham's determined support of their careers.

In the 90s, Durham elected to head for the hills, to Galisteo, some 20 minutes southeast of Santa Fe. What many perceived as a potentially disastrous abandonment of the Santa Fe scene has, on the contrary, proved that if one shows exceptional fine art, they will come – in droves. At this writing, Linda Durham has set a new precedent for Santa Fe dealers by acquiring a Manhattan exhibition space in the hot district of Chelsea. Over the years, Durham has from time to time collaborated with longtime New Mexico dealer Bunny Conlon, who will curate a show at Durham's new gallery.

At Gerald Peters' astounding 25,000 square foot gallery in Santa Fe, Gail Maxon, the gallery's Contemporary Art Director, has for many years championed a number of very fine New Mexico artists in her domain.

Minimalist art, by local artists and artists from throughout the world, found its most vociferous champion in dealer Charlotte Jackson. Jackson shares the distinction and the conviction of Linda Durham in annually exhibiting at the larger U.S. art fairs and regularly taking her shows overseas. Moreover, Jackson has spearheaded the four biennial ART Santa Fe fairs of the past decade.

Riva Yares, with her long experience and connections through her well-respected gallery in Arizona, eventually chose to bring her blue-chip stable to Santa Fe and, with Arlene LewAllen (whose LewAllen Contemporary Gallery succeeded the highly successful Elaine Horwitch Galleries in the 90s), became influential in significantly shifting the focus of the contemporary art scene to include downtown Santa Fe, hard by the Plaza. Arlene LewAllen, alone in Santa Fe, has vigorously pursued a regular program of showing established and up-and-coming African-American artists at her gallery.

Allene Lapides' very evolved and sophisticated taste was soon evident in her new extravagant Santa Fe space on Canyon Road where she champions local and national reputations.

Laura Carpenter, as noted earlier, can be credited with founding SITE Santa Fe. As a natural offshoot of her rigorously contemporary, often blue-chip stable, Carpenter brought to town exceptional, museum-quality works by key international abstract artists.

Any evaluation of the maturation of Santa Fe's art world at the turn of this new century has to take into serious account not only what art is created and shown here, but also what is *said* about it, around town and *entre nous*.

The all-important *dialogue* about art... "what is/is not 'art' in the new millennium? Or what art can 'be' or 'do' today? Or even 'tell me where is fancy bred, in the heart or in the head?'" has certainly shown healthy signs of intensity and some originality in the past decade.

What is *said* about art, both in public and around the dinner table or even over our constant cocktails, does seem of late to veer away from the customary Santa Fe "third largest art market" chatter (all too close to the equally tiresome Santa Fe real estate chatter) toward more substantive issues and answers.

Perhaps contributing most to this hesitant foray into art criticism and art *thinking* has been the superb lecturing programming mounted by, first and foremost, the Lannan Foundation and SITE Santa Fe. Both have invited major critics, writers and artists to speak and engage Santa Fe audiences on a level which anticipates that locals are not only ready for, but wholly up to the squirrelly issues in contemporary art. Again, what is nowadays *said* is perhaps the most encouraging phenomenon of all on the contemporary art scene.

Jan Ernst Adlmann

Jan Ernst Adlmann is a Santa Fe-based art consultant, art historian, and former museum director/curator (Vassar College, Long Beach, Assistant Director, Guggenheim Museum, New York City). He is also the author of Contemporary Art in New Mexico (1996).

INNOVATION

TAOS MODERNS

ANDREW DASBURG (1887-1979)
Winter Planes
Pastel, 1959
9¼ x 11"
Courtesy the Harwood Museum of Art

An important change occurred in the West's oldest art community during the 1940s. New artists arrived who did not accept the artistic conservatism for which Taos had been known. These artists were part of a larger wave of Modernism then sweeping the American art world. The Taos Moderns of the post-World War II era were not the first of their kind to invade the academic-romanticist turf held by conservative painters of wildlife, landscape, and Indians, but they did re-define the northern New Mexico art community. Some of the Modernists had come earlier; a few would not arrive until as late as the 1970s. The influence of Modernist thinking from New York (and thus from the imagery and traditions of Europe) and from San Francisco (informed by Asia and Asian religions) combined with the cultural and environmental influences of New Mexico. This created in the Southwest a variety of Modernism that remained intimately connected to the broader national currents of new thinking in art. The connection to the mainstream was not unique to the Taos

Moderns, as both earlier and later artists would also be a part of their respective times. But occurring as it did in an area remote from urban centers, this flowering of Modernism in Taos deserves extended comment.

No one could have anticipated that Taos would become a center for American Modernism after World War II. The shifting of the artistic center of gravity in the Western world from Europe to America in the 1940s had not been anticipated either – wanted, perhaps, and worked towards over a long period of time, but not, in advance of the event, a foregone conclusion. The twentieth, however, was the American century, and just as the balance of military, economic, and technological power shifted to the U.S., that this carried over into the realm of art seems less surprising in retrospect. What a change this was from two generations earlier. American artists of the late 19th century were anxious to create an American art that would stand in equal importance to that of Europe. Some of them thought it appropriate to follow the European model of setting up art colonies

LOUIS RIBAK (1903-1979)
Red & Black, c. 1970
Acrylic
60 x 47"
Courtesy Cline Fine Art

away from urban centers where artists could work from nature or study in the studio with established teachers. Some of the colonies, like that in Woodstock, New York, were not so far away. Others, like Taos, were physically remote.

Ernest Blumenschein, Victor Higgins, Walter Ufer and other members of the Taos Society of Artists (TSA) would create one of the most successful American art colonies. However, the history of Modernism in Taos was an equally important story running concurrently with that of the TSA academic romanticists. Several Modernists showed up in New Mexico following the first World War, the most important of whom, Marsden Hartley, stayed in Taos for half a year, then moved to Santa Fe for a while longer. He didn't like the art of the conservative Taos artists and he was too strange for their liking. Then other, but more congenial Modernists showed up.

Whatever he thought of the TSA's art with which he, as an artist, had nothing in common, Andrew Dasburg, between 1918 and 1979, would make himself an integral part of the Taos art scene and become the most venerable member of the art community. Over six decades he had become more than a fixture on the art scene: he had become the important link to the past of the art colony of the TSA, to the Taos Moderns, and to the very beginnings of American Modernism. He did not create the second era of the art community (that of the Taos Moderns, beginning in the 1940s) but he was there to foster it. When other modern artists arrived, they found in Dasburg not only a kindred spirit in his Modernist approach to art, but a progressive artist who had thrived in Taos and laid claim to it as a bastion of Modernism.

Louis Ribak and his wife Bea Mandelman, both painters, arrived from New York in 1944. Along with a few other residents such as Emil Bisttram (from 1930) and with Taos visitors – particularly Georgia O'Keeffe (from 1929) – this small group formed a nucleus around which the new artists arriving after World War II could coalesce. Not that this was in any sense an organized coalescing like the earlier TSA. This was more anarchic. Most of the moderns who arrived after 1945 did not know one another. For the most part, they knew little or nothing of the TSA (an exception was Agnes Martin, who somehow knew of them before coming to Taos). And when they arrived, they could not have guessed that so many would remain in New Mexico.

A decade of their era passed before the term "Taos Moderns" even appeared in print. But they did form a group identifiable, at least loosely, by their Modernist approach to art, however different their images were from one another. Janet Lippincott, a Santa Fe artist, studied in Taos with Emil Bisttram during 1949. As one of the very few moderns living in the capital city at the beginning of the 1950s, she was well known to the Taos Moderns. She stood out for being a female abstractionist. The Modernist community coalesced rapidly in the early 1950s. By the time of Dasburg's death, a few dozen artists had been associated in the loose grouping of the Taos Moderns. Together, they made Taos a crossroads of American Modernism between the major centers of New York and San Francisco.

This Modernist period in the history of the Taos art community was subject to several important external influences. The immediate one of Abstract Expressionism coming in from San Francisco (represented by Clyfford Still) and from New York (represented by Mark Rothko) was especially important. The New York School and their West Coast counterparts provided a model for how American artists could develop a truly American art. The possibilities of abstraction, even where figuration and subject matter re-emerged, finally became the model for a new American art.

For Taos and its new young artists, all this was something to grab onto. The academic romanticism of the TSA, like the politics of isolationism, no longer held much validity in the age of an unthinkably violent war just passed, and potentially worse ones to come. While big city artistic energy often turned to violent and unhappy themes (maybe a holdover from social realism), the Taos Moderns pursued an artistic course generally more serene and optimistic, tempered by the very different environment of New Mexico. It was their connection to the land that often differentiated their work from that being done in New York or even San Francisco.

Working out of New York, Hans Hoffmann provided a philosophical base that influenced how some of the Taos Moderns approached their new environment. Hoffmann asserted nature as the beginning point of artistic inspiration, "Whether the artist works directly from nature, from memory or from fantasy, nature is always the source of his creative impulses." He defined the artist as "an agent in whose mind nature is transformed." He even dealt with that other term so often used in conjunction with Taos artists: spirituality. Hoffmann described this as "the emotional and intellectual synthesis of relationships perceived in nature, rationally or intuitively." While Hoffmann never visited Taos, at least four of his students became Taos artists while many others were familiar with his teachings.

In San Francisco, Douglas McAgy presided over the California School of Fine Art, one the nation's most dynamic groups of artists. The art school provided a

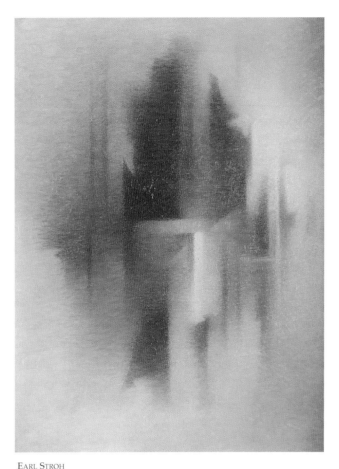

EARL STROH
Red Mirage
Oil
96 x 129cm
Courtesy the Harwood Museum of Art

stimulating environment not limited by the clock, remaining open twenty-four hours a day. In an era when numerous art schools sprang up to take advantage of the G.I. Bill – which paid students to attend classes – some of the most serious and progressive teachers found each other at this school. Despite the cross-continental flow of artists, the progressive painters of San Francisco maintained a separate identity from New York in the 1940s because of their further distance from Europe, and the natural tendency to look towards the Orient for inspiration. The glory days of the school ended in 1950 for a number of reasons, including restless artists who were by then ready to move on to other places and even to rebel against the art movement they had only just started. But also, politically conservative members of the school's board grew increasingly displeased with the new abstraction and pushed to return the school to emphasizing more familiar art forms. As had been true in New York, the creation of an uncomfortable climate in a big city directly benefited Taos. As the McAgy period sank, like Atlantis, it scattered its artist-provocateurs to the four winds. Its leading artist, Clyfford Still, moved to New York, while Richard Diebenkorn enrolled as a graduate student at the University of New Mexico in Albuquerque, and Edward Corbett and Clay Spohn joined the expanding group of Modernists in Taos.

The direct degree of influence of a particular artist on the Taos Moderns is hard to measure, but the art of Clyfford Still provided a model with direct implications for the nature-inspired painters in New Mexico. Still worked with naturalistic shapes that reflected rock, crystal, and land forms - forms which were American in character, but abstract rather than illustrative. Still denied any such connection, but the natural world provided an obvious basis for his brand of abstraction. If applying elements of both realistic and abstract to the same art seems a contradiction, it is also an example of how language fails to keep up with art. In Modernism, the representational may go beyond literal depiction to serve as something more. The landscape of mountains and sunsets becomes the landscape of psychology and morality, truth and beauty, the ultimate in natural realness to those who have the patience to get beyond the need for subject matter: art not just as religion, but art as deep spirituality.

Artists such as Still, Rothko, and Hoffmann showed that in making allusions to natural form, they could deal with romantic subject matter that need be neither literal-minded nor dull nor provincial. When Taos Moderns such as Corbett, Spohn, and Stroh moved beyond identifiable subject matter, they did so nonetheless influenced by the physical environment of northern New Mexico. The artistic influences of both New York and San Francisco proved critical to the type of thinking required to resist the seduction of an environment that pulled so many artists irresistibly into literal renderings. The difficulties of living in those urban environments just as irresistibly sent artists looking for a freer, less cluttered, and more natural living situation – just as it had for the first art colony denizens of two generations earlier.

The Taos Moderns, the best of them, brought a formal way of Modernist thinking to New Mexico. In the Southwest, they learned about new kinds of space and new kinds of light that they could translate in terms not just of subject, but of painting so that a unity of form and content could be achieved. They each accomplished that end in a different way. They did this outside of an urban setting, geographically far from big cities. The Taos Moderns made Taos their own at a time when many of the first immigrant artists had moved on, died, grown unproductive or at least moved past their best work. They created a second era for twentieth century art in Taos clearly distinguishable from the period that came before and that which came after.

Because of these new artists, Taos made the transition (not always smoothly) from the "art colony" of the first generation to an established, permanent presence on the American art scene. There are now more artists working in Taos than at any previous time, including many who continue working along paths blazed by earlier Modernists. By chance, the development phase of American Modernism ran roughly along the same period as Andrew Dasburg's association with Taos, 1918-1979. At its height in the 1950s, the Taos Moderns included a few dozen members. For a very small community, remote from all other art centers, to have had this ability to attract so many artists is nothing short of remarkable.

No one generalization can be made about the Taos Moderns except this: they purposely left urban life behind and, consciously or unconsciously, reflected or directly interpreted the power of the land in their art. They have not uncommonly described their art and its relation to the environment in Taoist terms. For these artists, creativity pervades life; it is in service to itself rather than in servitude to producing commodities. Taos goes its own way, producing art that is part of the larger American art mainstream, but with an unorthodox attitude derived from the harsh land and ancient cultures from which it has grown.

David L. Witt

Curator, The Harwood Museum of Art, Taos. Adapted from volume II, The Taos Moderns, by David L. Witt, the forthcoming art history from Red Crane Books.

VISION
AGNES MARTIN

Agnes Martin Gallery
Courtesy The Harwood Museum of Art

Until recently Agnes Martin has been this country's most famous unknown artist. Long a major figure in the international art world, she was less known in this country. A major 1992 retrospective at the Whitney Museum of American Art, a 1997 Golden Lion lifetime achievement award from La Biennale di Venezia, and designation by Art In America at the end of the 1990s as one of the world's leading artists has brought Martin higher visibility. Then, of course, there was also her 1994 one-person exhibition at the Harwood Museum in Taos. While this last accolade was less noticed than the others, the seven paintings in that show later constituted a permanent installation at the museum, the Taos version of the Rothko chapel. A show planned for 2002 at the Harwood will celebrate Martin's 90th birthday as well as a fifty-five year association with Taos. Her first showing at a museum was at the Harwood in 1947.

That show of University of New Mexico summer art school students received a brief newspaper review in which two artists were singled out: "Among the more advanced students, Agnes Martin and Earl Stroh have turned out some excellent work." The reviewer, let alone the artists, could not have known of the long and distinguished ties to Taos that would follow for both. Martin did not stay in Taos at that time but moved between New Mexico and New York until completing her art studies. By the time she returned to Taos in 1952, she was ready to settle in for five years of intensive studio work. She created as many as one hundred paintings during each of those years, but very few ever left her studio, and those mostly went to friends. Her Taos period compositions included many with fully abstract, biomorphic shapes. Perhaps because of their resemblance to the transitional phase of New York Modernist painting

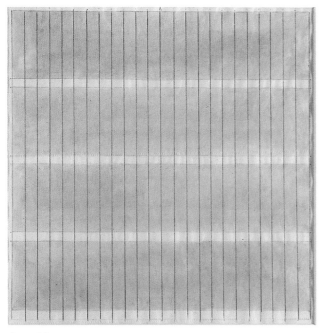

between Surrealism and Abstract Expressionism, she later destroyed all still in her possession. Fewer than ten paintings have survived from that five-year period.

These were impressively painted even if they did not achieve Martin's artistic goals. The shapes she presented in individual paintings appeared on the verge of forming themselves into something that might become recognizable, but their future evolution remained mysterious. Individual masses existed on the canvas without discernible commonalities yet clearly in relation to one another at the same time. American Modernism, especially in the years following World War II, placed a heavy emphasis on creating the new, but also on finding the underlying structure, be it something physical or an idea, which held reality together. Martin set herself the task of finding a way to express this visually.

She showed this work to New York art impresario Betty Parsons whose gallery had developed star-making power. Parsons apparently visited Taos more than once. Like other Abstract Expressionists, Martin was highly ambitious to create the new in American art while being at the same time wary of success. Success inevitably meant recognition and celebrity, neither of which the

reclusive artist seemed ready to court. This package for the contemporary artist, however, is one that is unavoidable. By 1955, Martin was showing with Parsons and two years later moved to New York. After she was there for a time, she came upon the idea of the grid. In its various manifestations from simple pencil lines to deceptively complex paintings, it made her reputation internationally. She has given two accounts of its development. One was that she wanted to create something that she thought no one would want. This statement is not flippant but in keeping with the Modernist ideology of the New York School as well as the Taos Moderns. Creating the new, and thus the not-yet-accepted, was the goal of artistic creation. Simultaneously, the artists craved acceptance for their work – few artists ever worked so hard as did the New York School to make themselves such a dominating artistic force. They could not reconcile this paradox, but non-rational reasoning is as good a motivator as any other. Abstract Expressionism (a motley collection of dissimilar Late Modernist approaches, having more in common for being of the same time period than for stylistic commonalities) of course could not remain forever new and thus, by the logic of its own creators, could not remain permanently valid.

The other, more recent account Martin gave was her twenty-year search to create an art that was truly abstract. She told me, "I was thinking about innocence. The first [abstract] painting I liked I showed to the Museum of Modern Art and they bought it. In 1959. They still show it. For some reason it is called *The Tree...* but it is really about innocence." Paintings in her studio in March 2001, reflecting similar themes, were titled with such names as Benevolence and Peace and Happiness. "I call that one Happy Holiday," she said, pointing to one of them. "Does it look like a happy holiday to you?"

Martin is "fussy about scale," as she states it, and the composition of each painting is carefully measured in her head and on pages of paper filled with arcane mathematical calculations. The work is not about mathematics. The math is just a way into making sure that the proportions she imagined will be realized on canvas. This is essential because the way we respond to a work of art, she believes, is the way we learn about ourselves. This learning is the purpose of art: "There is a wider range of emotion that is the response to abstract feelings. These don't get enough attention. Art makes concrete these abstract incidents so they can be responded to. An abstract response is a response to something you can't put your finger on as the cause. There is a happiness without a cause. It is this that I try to illustrate."

This philosophical aspect of Martin is a factor that distinguishes her from many other artists. Holding a belief in the transcendental and eternal, but with no apparent allegiance to religion, she speaks of truth, beauty, and happiness as the elements of reality that are there to be seen and experienced for those open to doing so. Although several Taos Moderns claimed to have been influenced by Taoism and related Asian tenets, Martin put this way of being in the world into her art more consciously than perhaps any other artist.

Although she disclaims the term "spirituality" in describing her painting, at the same time the work represents her expression of that which is timeless and in some ways formless. This flow (or system) of perception, she believes, surrounds us as a kind of ether, linking us in a commonality. It would be tempting to call this a commonality of "spirit," but that would take on the religious connotations that Martin rejects. This esoteric approach, with roots in Taoism, sounds odd to those trained to think primarily in empirical terms. The contradiction of depicting a narrative-less story is nearly beyond the ability of words. Story refers to the quality of conveying meaning. This meaning can be as direct, and at the same time as elusive, as conveying an artist's conception of truth and beauty. The highly rational (even mathematical), non-objective world of Martin's paintings is filled with meaning but not with narrative subject matter. Her art is about intuitively felt emotions, emotional response along the lines of the beauty and passion one might hear in symphonic music.

Depicting meaning in the absence of subject has always been the conundrum of abstract art for artists, and finding the meaning of a composition without clear guideposts has always been the difficulty for viewers. Art that is clearly of its time, but which also transcends its time to hold meaningfulness for viewers of later times, is the important criteria for judging what is or is not successful. Martin's work may go on to meet this test in future centuries. In the meantime, what are we to make of Martin's super-rational approach to depicting the deepest level of emotion? This is the art of detached passion, meditative but not religious, static like the unified form of a waterfall at a distance, but also fluid like the elusive movement of a single drop as it careens within the fall seen up close. The straightness of a line or the position of a subtle color passage which seemed clearly placed at a distance in Martin's paintings often (seemingly) shifts position or disappears altogether upon the near approach.

Whether or not one accepts the belief in the ether of truth and beauty that Martin feels surrounds us, the sheer technical confidence of the painting is presented as evidence of its existence. Her work is not the kind that gives instantaneous visual satisfaction. The intensely worked paintings demonstrate a subtlety that her admirers love and that others sometimes cannot see at all. Martin's painting is not exactly about nature since that approach would put subject matter or narrative into it, but it is about emotions at the deepest level, the place from where meaning arises, the state of basic organization. This is not the nature of weather, landscapes, and life forms, but the nature beneath the nature, the organizational principles upon which all else rests.

Adapted from Volume II, The Taos Moderns, by David L. Witt, the forthcoming art history from Red Crane Books.
©2001 David L. Witt

DIALOGUE

SITE SANTA FE   A BRIEF HISTORY

Gajin Fujita, *Beau Monde*, 2000,
designed for SITE Santa Fe's Fourth International Biennial

The essential thing to grasp is that there really is no SITE at all in the usual sense – even though it has an address and a staff, and occasionally creates controversy – for nothing is sited at SITE. SITE is all form and no content, which is to say that it gathers contemporary art only to disperse it. At the end of the great age of collecting in America (think: Mellon, Lehman, Gardner, Barnes, Simon, etc.), SITE collects nothing at all.

This odd arrangement offers dramatic advantages because SITE Santa Fe is not shackled to a past. Never having begun collecting, it is not obliged to continue, nor will it be lured into faddish dead ends. Instead, SITE remains alert to the moment, able to reinvent itself continuously, to give its all, literally, to whatever it exhibits, accommodating artists in dramatic ways. Its space becomes plastic as walls are put up, taken down, cut through to create windows. So perhaps one should say SITE has no content and hardly any form.

How did this different kind of art center arise, and what has it got to do with Santa Fe, the "city different?" In 1993, a determined group of art aficionados wanted to expand the city's art offerings. True, they reasoned, Santa Fe had a thriving art market, offering serious and varied work alongside the inevitable lurid landscapes and sheep's skulls. Nonetheless, the founders believed

that the town deserved and would support exposure to the most engaging and challenging art of the day, wherever in the world it was made and in whatever medium. So at a time when multisited installations by international artists were hot, the founders proposed a temporary show, at selected venues across town, of work never before seen in Santa Fe – but work that, in contemporary ways, would respond to the legacy of Native American and Spanish Colonial culture, landscape, tourism, and Anglo heritage.

Before it was even born, SITE sparked debate. Some intelligent and well-meaning voices complained of exclusivity and condescension and questioned the project's necessity. Don't we already have access to a wide variety of contemporary art, they wondered, so why slight the work done here? Why "SLITE Santa Fe?" Also, the City balked at the idea of placing art all over town.

Such obstacles failed to dissuade the founders, especially after someone remembered an empty beer distribution warehouse on the edge of the railyard. With its concrete floors and industrial ceilings, it already resembled contemporary exhibition spaces. If Frank Gehry had turned a warehouse into Los Angeles' highly successful Museum of Contemporary Art, why not here? So, after finding resources to match their passion, these founders commissioned the New York architect Richard Gluckman to reconfigure the 18,000 square foot space, and they hired Bruce W. Ferguson to curate the inaugural exhibition.

In 1995, SITE Santa Fe's first biennial, *Longing and Belonging: From the Faraway Nearby*[1], explored ways that self and place relate. From 13 countries, Ferguson brought 31 artists, both unknowns and well-knowns like Ann Hamilton, Anish Kapoor, Bruce Nauman, Jenny Holzer, and Trinh T. Minh-ha. Their installation-oriented works were specific to the artists' experiences in New Mexico, or to the state's history, notably Meridel Rubenstein's glass house with video of Robert Oppenheimer, which reminded viewers that *Longing and Belonging*

---

[1]This subtitle was the closing salutation that Georgia O'Keeffe used in writing to East Coast friends. As New Mexico's most famous link to the international scene, her heritage has haunted the biennials, most wittily in Maurizio Cattelan's giant walking puppet in 1997.

Installation view: Foreground: Jennifer Steinkamp and Jimmy Johnson, *sin(time)*, 2001, DVD projection, curved wall, sound, 96½ x 312 x 96½ inches. Commissioned by SITE Santa Fe. Background: Alexis Smith, *Red Carpet*, 2001, mixed-media installation with landscape wall painting and hand-tufted, New Zealand-wool area rug. Rug dimensions: 25 feet x 34½ feet x ½ inches. Commissioned by SITE Santa Fe. Photo: Herbert Lotz. SITE Santa Fe's Fourth International Biennial, July 14, 2001 - January 6, 2002

opened on the 50th anniversary of detonating the first atomic bomb. In SITE-less fashion, Rubenstein's work was installed at the Museum of Fine Arts, along with several other pieces in the biennial. Still more work appeared at a downtown restaurant, at the Palace of the Governors, and at the Greer Garson Theater.

Following the biennial, a shift crucial to SITE's history occurred: cause and effect changed places and the container became the contained. Initially, SITE was conceived simply to facilitate a show; thereafter, it was to fold its tents or hibernate until the second biennial. (Optimistic, of course: the title "first biennial" showed moxie, since no one had guaranteed that a second would follow.) However, because Ferguson's show generated so much excitement, both publicly and critically, and because Gluckman's renovations proved so workable, the board elected to keep SITE open year round in a *Kunsthalle* format with ongoing exhibitions, and hired Ferguson as its first director. So this nomadic organization acquired a permanent address, where it has installed

some 35 projects to date. The challenge was to transform an organization defined by international shows into a permanent space mounting exhibits meaningful to its community – like Patrick McFarlin's on-site portrait studio, or a robotics show mounted in consultation with the Los Alamos labs – while retaining its international profile. When Ferguson left in 1996 to head the New York Academy of Art, that challenge fell to the new director, Louis Grachos, previously curator of the San Diego Museum of Contemporary Art.

A double rhythm was thereby established, biennials alternating with shows devoted to an individual (Juan Muñoz, Allan Graham), a theme (abstraction), or a medium (video). While biennials make bigger splashes, these two rhythms are in sync, because the alternating shows display new works from New Mexico, the nation, and the world, and offer emerging and established artists exposure and publications.

SITE's second biennial, *TRUCE: Echoes of Art in an Age of Endless Conclusions*, benefited from the concurrent

North façade of SITE Santa Fe, Installation view of Graft Design's *Kissy Kissy Touchy Touchy*, 2001, artificial flora, dimensions variable. Courtesy of the artists. Commissioned by SITE Santa Fe; and Jim Isermann's *Untitled (0101) (silver)*, 2001, painted vacuum formed ABS plastic, 24 x 24 x 3 inches each (750 panels), façade dimensions: 24 x 113 x 5½ feet. Courtesy of the artist; Corvi-Mora, London; Feature Inc., New York; and Richard Telles Fine Art, Los Angeles. Partially commissioned by SITE Santa Fe. Photo: Herbert Lotz. SITE Santa Fe's Fourth International Biennial, July 14, 2001 - January 6, 2002.

opening of the Georgia O'Keeffe Museum as well as the second ART Santa Fe contemporary art fair, producing a triple header that attracted the art world's attention. Aptly named, this biennial signaled a truce with the community by engaging in dialogues with local voices. Curator Francesco Bonami assembled 27 artists from 20 countries whose work connected isolated individuals to communal forces and contested our culture's language of violence as "the only transmitter of meaning." Among this biennial's successes count Sam Taylor-Wood's simultaneous videos of five isolated people narrating their lives, Esko Männikkö's bleak photographs of West Texas Hispanic communities, subREAL's documenting of Ceaucescu's fall, and, in his first U.S. showing, William Kentridge's animations of post-apartheid South Africa.

In 1999, Rosa Martínez extended the earlier biennials' meditations on place by bringing 29 artists from 23 countries together in *Looking for a Place*. Understanding her role as editor/agitator, Martínez wanted a "fluid alternative to the inviolable solidity of museums," where white cubes display beautiful objects. So her artists both punctured SITE's walls and reached beyond them into public, commercial, and sacred spaces like the old dancehall at Galisteo, the Los Alamos airport, and a municipal parking garage. Nobody objected to Diller + Scofidio's multimedia installation in Room 120 of the Budget Inn, but even after permissions were granted, two installations – the cemetery for a Hispanic Catholic parish church and a lake on a nearby Indian Pueblo – were dismantled in the opening days, rather speeding up the biennial's ephemeral quality. (That these works made trouble when they were inserted into sacred spaces demonstrates anew how art takes on a semi-sacred character in today's culture, despite the curators' efforts to demystify that aura.) In fact, the most memorable installation was housed inside SITE's building: Iranian artist Shirin Neshat's double video about sexual segregation and conflict in Islamic culture.

Not satisfied simply to mount exhibitions, SITE added an impressive collection of public, educational, and outreach programs, further integrating this artspace into the community. They include the Young Curators and Young Critics Programs and the *Art & Culture* lecture and performance series. Not to mention collaborations with the Santa Fe Chamber Music Festival, the Santa Fe Institute, Challenge New Mexico, the Children's Museum, and the Santa Fe Art Institute. Such well attended programs further enrich the life of a community already dense with cultural offerings, and address underserved populations from pueblos to public schools.

In selecting Dave Hickey to curate its fourth biennial, SITE made a bold and canny choice because Hickey had vociferously criticized both the concept and execution of biennials as "trade shows for curators in search of internationally certified installations to fill out their exhibition schedules." While the earlier curators all scoured the globe in search of artists to weave installations around a loose theme, Hickey opted for the pragmatic, the democratic, and the historical in *Beau Monde: Toward a Redeemed Cosmopolitanism*. Instead of trying to make an ideological point, he organized "an exhibition that I want to *see*," whose fundamental criterion was simply "Does the space look better and more interesting with or without it?" Hickey selected 27 international artists, including Jo Baer, Ed Ruscha, Jesús Rafael Soto, and Jessica Stockholder, who wove diverse cultural milieux into a "*beau monde.*"

"Cosmopolitanism?" The Berlin/L.A. firm of Graft Design effaced all institutional and geographical traces of SITE and of Santa Fe: no logo, no historic-district regulation brown stucco. With Jim Isermann's 750 plastic panels made to look like aluminum sheathing, Gajin Fujita's graffitied wraparound mural, and Graft Design's wooden ramp flanked by fake sunflowers, we could have been many places, especially Las Vegas.

Hickey's biennial was more coherent architecturally than his predecessors': for example, the ramp that led visitors into the building and seemed to emerge on the back side beyond a big new window. With the repeating concave curves and the alternating rhythm of large and small rooms, the space interconnected so effectively that people called the revamped building Hickey's own *Gesamtkunstwerke*, or artwork, the various installations like strokes on his canvas. (For a change, this biennial featured lots of painting.)

Coherence welcomed diversity, and part of *Beau Monde's* fun was connecting the dots. Hickey's Principle: everything relates to something else, and nothing relates to everything. In a New York-style room that seemed to come straight out of the Museum of Modern Art – white walls, gray carpet, high ceilings – Hickey hung four Ellsworth Kelly canvases across from four Kenneth Price biomorphic sculptures, each gaining punch thanks to the contrast. Between the Kellys and the Prices a large passageway functioned as a kind of frame that enclosed a gold wallpapered passage (Vegas again); which then enclosed part of Takashi Murakami's superflat, post-Pop, happyface wallpaper; which enclosed, finally, a mottled magenta wall on which hung Jeff Burton still photos from "adult entertainment" films. (Among the most graphically arresting works in the show, his photos were worlds apart from the high formalist Kelly and Price, even as all three artists mixed up the sexy and the sculptural.)

Beau Monde provoked many debates about Hickey's selections, but such thumb-upping and -downing served his abiding interest in community. Differences in taste create cliques, prompting conversation and thereby weaving a cosmopolitan community of people talking to each other across fault lines of generation or upbringing. Hickey also dialogued with his predecessors. While the first three biennials all mounted some form of political critique by artists roughly the same age making related statements, *Beau Monde*, by contrast, oriented itself aesthetically and traced artistic influences across generations.

Hickey's "*beau*," or beautiful, isn't pretty. Instead it comprises unfamiliar and disturbing elements, so that visual pleasure necessarily carries an element of anxiety, strangeness, pain. (This element Hickey regards as vestiges of an originary violence that art functions to sublimate.) Therefore an aesthetics of queasiness runs through this biennial: Jennifer Steinkamp's dizzying vibrations of light and line; ditto Soto's that, as you walked past, could turn your stomach; Pia Fries's wooden panels loaded with sculpted paint in "tasteless," glaring colors, so excessively luscious and over the top as to cloy; and more. Hickey framed them all in engaging spaces, where viewers could tolerate this unsettling "beauty."

Did Hickey escape his own critique and resist the gravitational pull of the biennial agenda? Or was he compromised or co-opted into some more or less uneasy truce with convention? The critic-turned-curator had painted himself into a corner, but he got out in good American pragmatist fashion – not by theoretically outflanking or outsmarting his critics, but precisely by *curating*. Hickey wanted a fun and provocative show, and he put it together, a biennial that generated energy enough to send SITE into a new, sometimes wobbly, orbit.

For an artspace just six years old, SITE Santa Fe has established an extensive network of roots that connect it with many aspects of the community, and, in turn, connect that community to the art world at large. The founders fashioned a SITE to behold, well sited in Santa Fe.

Arden Reed

Arden Reed, professor of English at Pomona College, is the author of Talking Pictures: Manet, Flaubert, and the Emergence of Modernism, *forthcoming from Cambridge University Press.*

ESSENCE

BILL BARRETT

Untitled Model, 2001
Cast bronze, unique
17"H x 21"W x 18"D

Recent works of Bill Barrett move with grace and vitality. Their origins are deeper than the dancers and movements they so clearly evoke. Rodin, Henry Moore, the Futurists all had an influence on Barrett, and here one gets a glimpse of Degas. The more profound influences have come from two-dimensional art: expressionism, Asian calligraphy and, deepest of all, surrealism. Surrealism as process rather than image; surrealism as access to the locus of memory and feeling, to the place where the human inclination to sing and to move gracefully has its origins.

Representing the evanescent in bronze is no mean feat. For Barrett it took 40 years of refining technique to the point where technique could disappear in works that were as much essence as object. His enabling invention starts with his drawing forms freely in wax. He selects and combines these elements into free-standing wax models, the best of which are cast in bronze. The larger versions he fabricates – impeccably – from bronze sheet. Through it all, the expressive freedom of drawing is retained but, inevitably, the process is influenced by temperament. How lucky we are that this sculptor's temperament, in defiance of the aesthetic rules of the age, avoids the dark places of our subconscious to create works of verve and harmony and, in the ultimate act of defiance, of sheer beauty.

Philip F. Palmedo, author of the forthcoming book, *Bill Barrett, The Life of a Sculptor*

BILL BARRETT
Aladdin, 2000
Fabricated bronze
60"H x 57"W x 57"D

CLARITY

NEW MEXICO GLASS IN CONTEXT

New Mexico has long been a haven for artists. The majestic vistas and always-blue skies attract them; many now use glass in their work. Like a bold and bright Southwest sky, glass seduces with reflecting light. Glass is versatile; it can be clear or opaque, fluid or solid. With heat, glass can be manipulated by many techniques including bending, blowing, and casting. When glass is cold and solid, gluing, coating and polishing can refine it.

The magic of transparency has tempted artists to explore and push the boundaries – just like their predecessors did. In the 1840s, Hispanic metalworkers collected discarded cans and hammered the tin into devotional items embedding shards of painted glass. A century later, in the 1930s and '40s, Florence Pierce joined the Transcendental Painting Group in Taos. In 1970, she started pouring polyester resin onto mirrored Plexiglas to create paintings, which she named "light bodies." She was using modern technology to make luminous paintings. Their essence is transparency and reflection.

Larry Bell, an eclectic sculptor, is also fascinated by light. The artist began experimenting with attaching glass to canvas in 1962 about a decade before he settled in Taos. In California he constructed glass cubes. He wanted a reflective surface on both sides of the glass so he coated the sheets with metal, in effect creating non-pigment light interference color or "mirrorizing" them. With these, he created glass environments so large viewers could walk into them. They look like translucent cubes within cubes. "Light is Bell's chosen medium; illusion, then, is the magic that makes it perform," wrote Douglas Kent Hall in *Zones of Experience: The Art of Larry Bell*. Bell also makes vapor drawings using similar technology to create reflective surfaces on paper that transmits light.

Studio glass: During that same decade, an exuberant studio glass movement started gaining credibility in other parts of the country. Harvey Littleton, the son of a physicist for Corning Glass Works in western New York, is credited with this question: "Might hot glass evolve more as art than craft if it could be produced in an artist's studio rather than in a factory?" To test this notion, in 1962, Littleton, then a professor at the University of Wisconsin, organized a glass blowing workshop with the help of the Toledo Museum of Art. Furnaces small enough to fit individual studios evolved from that, allowing Littleton's students and colleagues to build hot shops for campuses and workshops. In 1964 Marvin Lipofsky started the glass program at UC Berkeley. Then in 1967, he started the Glass Department at California College of Arts and Crafts (CCAC). Many other important

HARVEY LITTLETON – 1968
Classic Symbol
Blown glass
28 x 10½ x 11"

FLO PERKINS – 2001
Pas de Trois Couleurs
Glass, steel, bronze
42 x 34 x 29"
Courtesy LewAllen Contemporary

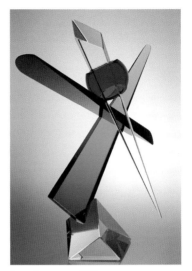

JOHN BINGHAM - 2001
Untitled
Blown & fabricated glass
21 x 18 x 11"

EMILY BROCK
Wet Paint, detail
Cast, slumped & fabricated kiln work
15½D x 18W x 18"T

HENRY SUMMA - 2001
Solar Ring
Blown & fabricated glass
6 x 6 x 6"

programs were also established. The enthusiasm was contagious. Young ceramicists, sculptors and painters changed their majors to work in glass. The studio glass movement had become a fully realized entity.

Lacking master glass blowers to guide them, Americans produced what their European counterparts called "free glass," rambunctious creativity flowing with and from the nationwide irreverence of the '60s. Unlike European factories where workers blow a designer's creation, the Americans were the glass blowers, the designers, and in most cases, the technicians that built the equipment. Ironically though, even such adventurousness was not enough to shatter glass blowers' early reliance on forms more familiar to crafts than art. A fundamental debate continues: is glass craft or art?

Despite the debate, a phalanx of museum organizers, journal critics, gallery owners and collectors determinedly backed the idea of glass as art. Three events helped to increase this excitement. In 1966, The Toledo Museum of Art staged a "Glass National" invitational exhibition, unleashing a frenzy of symposia and meetings. The Glass Art Society (GAS) was organized in 1970 by artists Fritz Dreisbach and Mark Peiser. The meeting, a year later,

had a small group of glassmakers – 21 men, and 1 woman. Members of the society now number 3,350 from 48 countries. The Corning Museum of Glass promoted international awareness with its "New Glass: A Worldwide Survey" in 1979. That exhibition made evident the numerous ways glass was being used; hot glass shops that blew vessels, warm glass involving kiln work, and cold worked glass.

Hot glass: New Mexico's studio-glass movement began in earnest in the late '60s when glass blowers Mel Knowles and Jack Miller enticed customers to Santa Fe with an open-air studio. When Peter VanderLaan bought the studio-showroom in 1969, the Glory Hole Glassworks' colleagues continued to hone their skills. The studio attracted a network of artists such as Henry Summa, Peet Robison, Charlie Miner, John Bingham, Wayne Archer, and Jenny Langston, each contributing new information. While Miner eventually started Tesuque Glassworks, another hot shop open to the public, others preferred private studios out of the spotlight. At present, Liquid Light, a hot shop on Santa Fe's Baca Street owned by Elodie Holmes, keeps the open studio tradition alive

LARRY BELL – 1995
6x 6-4-AB
12MM glass/coated with inconal
1997 Exhibition
Bergen Museum of Art, Norway

by hosting demonstrations with internationally known artists. Another Santa Fe shop is Connie Christopher's Haute Glass on Second Street.

VanderLaan, known for his highly colorful work, and his wife, artist Mary Beth Bliss, known for her reflective optical glass, recently relocated their gallery back to Canyon Road with plans to reopen their hot shop there. Miner, of Tesuque, creates impressively large cast platters circled by a fish relief in pale blues and greens. Summa, of Santa Fe, concentrates on intensely complex marbles, paperweights and multicolored vessels. Sometimes, as in "Solar Ring," he glues blown elements together. Bingham combines glassblowing with cut and polished glass. His work with Karen Hastings contrasts geometric shapes with fluid forms in which light and balance are playful yet beautiful elements similar to "Untitled." (Illustrated)

Glass as tradition: Even older traditions emerge when Pueblo leaders endorse glasswork as a valid expansion of native culture. Glass water vessels by C.J. Tarpley replicate age-old Pueblo pottery, sometimes incorporating abstract San Idlefonso designs. Tony Jojola, of Isleta

Pueblo, taps a tribal passion for pottery to create glass that mimics woven baskets. He traces his earliest experience with glass to 1975, when he fired up a defunct glass furnace previously built by Dale Chihuly at the Indian School in Santa Fe. In 1998, with Chihuly's backing, Jojola built a glass shop in Taos to develop a mentoring program for youths. Native Americans have long been admired for colorful beadwork; Marcus Amerman, of Santa Fe, continues this tradition. He recreates 19th century photos of Native Americans with his beadwork in combination with paint on canvas or sometimes stitched on clothing.

Lampwork: While some glassmakers practice on a large scale others focus small. Arno Foensch was a respected master lampworker in Los Alamos from the Manhattan Project days, when he made precision scientific glass; Wayne Archer, with multiple talents, continues the tradition. Lewis Wilson, of Albuquerque, promotes beadmaking through his videos and classes at Crystal Myths. He also organizes bead-making symposiums in New Mexico, Arizona and Hawaii.

Kiln formed glass: In the late 60's, stained-glass artists emerged as part of the nation's back-to-the-country fervor. *Glass Studio* magazine helped to fuel that interest. In Albuquerque, artists Ruth and Norman Dobbins organized workshops that introduced kiln-working techniques. They also taught sandblasting to create relief designs in glass. One artist, Emily Brock, living in New Mexico since 1976, was inspired by their workshops. Her art is difficult to categorize. She makes miniature environments that are perfect in every detail, using almost every glass technique presently known. Cast figures are now placed in structured settings, as in "Wet Paint."

New Directions: In l983, the Tucson Museum of Art, led by Suzanne K. Frantz, organized the country's first exhibition of sculptural glass and included several Southwest artists. Valerie Arber made a large colorful fused-glass flag installation. Mary Shaffer contributed "Path," a 30-foot slumped glass installation that OK Harris Gallery in New York displayed in 1980 along with "Waterfall." Flo Perkins, of Pojoaque, set up a cactus garden of glass. She now makes 5-foot sculptures of wrought iron, cast bronze and delicately blown cactus blossoms. Her work, full of motion, is as windswept as the Southwest.

MARY SHAFFER
Waterfall - 1982
Slumped glass
108" x 108" x 72"
O.K. Harris, New York, NY

Dale Chihuly started Pilchuck Glass School, devoted solely to glass, in Seattle in l971. It has been an important center for the exchange of ideas and for turning artists into lifelong friends. Most important, however, was its mission to promote glass as art. In the 70's, Italo Scanga and Mary Shaffer were among the first artists-in-residence invited because they already used glass in their work. Later, artists like Kiki Smith and Linda Bengalis (both part time New Mexico residents) were invited to nurture their interest in using glass as a medium.

There are many more artists in New Mexico using glass for sculpture, and many more pursuing their interest in craft. Whatever the route, artists in the Southwest welcome the sense of place. The setting – high altitudes, huge skies, harsh desert, warm colors – inspires them. Bingham, who works amid rolling hills of juniper and piñon trees outside Santa Fe, applauds the region's "solitude and serenity." Natives emerge from seclusion, or transplants arrive as loners doing solitary explorations meaningful to them. In pursuit of individual visions, some create with an exuberance of color and others refine glass to its essence of clarity and transparency.

Written and researched by Maiya Keck, Alice Klement

PARADOX

FRITZ SCHOLDER

FRITZ SCHOLDER
Indian with Umbrella
Acrylic on canvas
80 x 68"

Native Americans of the 1960s and 70s were living their own paradox: an ancient people with centuries of tradition and culture, struggling to retain their unique identity while being assimilated into a gobbling Anglo society that controlled and devalued them at every turn. At this moment, Scholder came face to face with his first personal paradox: an Indian looking from the perspective of a non-Indian upon an Indian.

In 1967, almost against his own will, Fritz Scholder painted an Indian. After three years in Santa Fe during which he had painted mostly landscapes and butterflies, he began a series, *Indian*, which would not end until 1980, thirteen years and hundreds of paintings later. He could not have imagined that it would be he who broke the mold in portraying the American Indian in his contemporary, socio-political reality. He used a modern approach that revolutionized traditional attitudes toward Indian art and won him widespread recognition.

He painted an abstracted landscape, which all the tribes in the area shared, and added contemporary Indian images. Scholder wrote, "It just naturally came about that I realized that I had to paint the subject – and the minute I did, I was surprised by the uproar that came about because I had realized that the subject needed to be brought into a contemporary mode... The older Indians felt that I, in some way, was against Indians."

Scholder has said, "In a way I am a paradox. I have changed the direction of so-called Indian painting, but I don't consider myself an Indian painter. I have painted the Indian real *not* red" is how he describes it, and in doing so he has presented a new frame of reference in which to think of and envision these indigenous peoples. Scholder's breakthrough, which began the New Indian Art Movement, unleashed a torrent of heretofore unseen images by T.C. Cannon, Earl Biss, Robert Penn, Linda Lomahaftewa and Jaune Quick-To-See Smith, among others. American Indian art had freed itself from the impositions put upon by it by Anglo-European standards of "academic" painting.

After 1980 Scholder began to paint other subjects, and in doing so redefined his artistic identity as a

Fritz Scholder, internationally known for his uniquely untraditional and unsentimental depictions of Native Americans, presents himself in a precarious, yet seemingly comfortable balance between the Anglo world and the world of the Indian of the late twentieth century. Born in 1937 in rural Minnesota, Scholder grew up as a non-Indian. Not until 1961 at a Southwest Indian Art Project did he publicly and proudly present himself as an Indian (the California Luiseño tribe). In 1964 he accepted an invitation from Lloyd Kiva New to join the faculty at the newly-established Institute of American Indian Arts in Santa Fe.

"It was a new experience to know Indians. They seemed exotic and very different," he says. As different as they may have seemed, Scholder noticed that everyone there painted Indians and only Indians. He vowed at the time never to paint an Indian.

FRITZ SCHOLDER
Not Alone #11
Oil on canvas
46 x 36″

FRITZ SCHOLDER
Not Alone #16
Acrylic on canvas
30 x 40"

painter of portraits, landscapes and still life. A highly original talent, Scholder is a painter first, but as a creative persona he is also photographer, poet, printmaker, sculptor and world traveler. Particularly drawn to Egypt, he has long been interested in the area, which is seen as a source in his paintings.

At work, Scholder paints mainly at night. In his studio he prepares the canvas carefully and then works with strength and sureness in his brushstrokes, applying his strong colors in bold quick movements. It is as if he is possessed, a shaman full of magic; images leave their third dimensional realm and jump into the two dimensional world of the canvas.

Over a period of forty-plus years, Scholder has continually elevated his style of painting and his dramatic expressionistic use of color. Writing about his friend

Andy Warhol, Scholder said, "I realized he was very courageous by choosing subjects which no other artist would touch – like the electric chair, Marilyn, dollar bills, Mickey Mouse and soup cans. I realized that no subject is bad if you approach it and make it your own." In praise of Fritz Scholder, his friend Lloyd Kiva New wrote, "Scholder opened up a whole new world of painting to Indian artists. His attitude toward making art has revolutionized the approach of Native artists, moving the art from clichés to personal, often expressionistic statements. The great barrier has come down. Scholder has helped Indian artists find their voices, and thus, their personal artistic freedoms."

Patrizia Kaye
Santa Fe based writer and publisher

JAMES HAVARD

WOMAN IN THE RIO GRANDE

Oil on canvas
67 x 51"

James Havard came to Santa Fe in a roundabout way, beginning as a young aspiring rancher, then gaining a reputation as an important New York artist. Today, he is a truly original painter whose work is at once spontaneous and polished, primitive and sophisticated, mysterious and immediate. Havard's academic skill, combined with his robust style and his freedom of thought, forges unforgettable images. As an influential artist who took his art outside the current trends altogether, he has risen even further in the eyes of the international collectors and critics who recognize his work.

SETH ANDERSON

IN A SINGLE BOUND

Seth Anderson's career as an artist began during a 1993 fellowship at the Glasgow School of Art in Glasgow, Scotland. His work stems from "doodling" and "taping" into the subconscious. Shapes and forms are created from scribbles and reactions, without attention toward a specific subject. The work is aimed at movement, emotion, and weight, while reflecting the mind and soul of the artist. At twenty-nine years of age, Anderson is no longer an emerging artist, having completed six one-person and nine group exhibitions. His work has been collected extensively throughout the United States and abroad. Anderson grew up in New Mexico and continues to live and work in this beautiful state.

Mixed media on wood
60 x 60 x 3"

SALLY ANDERSON

OLD GOLD

Mixed media on wood
24 x 40½ x 5"

Sally Anderson has lived and worked in New Mexico for the last thirty years. Using a variety of painting techniques applied to sheets of Mylar and ultimately bonded to wood, aluminum, or bronze, Anderson creates mixed media works somewhere between painting and sculpture. These immaculately rendered works are created from years of experimentation in fiber art, painting, and product design, and represent a personal journey of gathering, reflection and discovery.

VALDEZ ABEYTA Y VALDEZ

THE THIRD STONE AND THE FIFTH REED

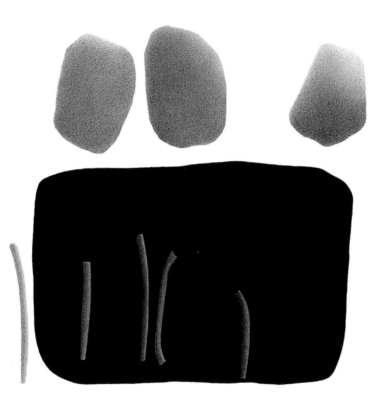

Colored pencil
29¼ x 35½"

Valdez Abeyta y Valdez. In her earliest memory, she walks beside her grandmother while seeds fall from her grandmother's hand from far above her head. She remembers the silence of the garden and the sound the seeds made as they fell to the earth. Valdez Abeyta y Valdez hears a drawing before she draws it – the muted measure of a hoe on the earth, the sharp echo of rock against rock in spring runoff, the clicking of castanets as a flamenco dancer walks past a loud construction site, the call of an owl at dusk.

Valdez, outside in her yard, all of it her garden, thinks, "If I had been a woman living a hundred years ago and my work was outside in fields and gardens, I would have been content. I would have been happy." Silence and sound are her inspiration. Seven hours a day she translates the silence of grade school classrooms into six hundred small hands beating, drumming. Thundering. Her three daughters, too, are her own heart beating, her loves.

Drawing, Valdez enters the silence of paper and the paper sings with the sounds she hears. Guzman, the artist, says of her drawings, "They are things that you can't get a grip on but they hold on to you."

MARY SHAFFER

TRIANGLE ANCHOR

Mary Shaffer turned from painting to glass in the early 1970s, responding to its versatility as well as its expressive appeal. Almost from the start, she drew acclaim for a mid-air slumping technique she developed that shaped glass by retaining heat and relying on gravity.

Concerned with content, not function or surface beauty, Shaffer began a sculptural movement within the world of glass that resonates today. Working with every form of the material from fiber optics, plate glass, and hot glass, she has fashioned intimate objects, filled rooms with narrative-driven installations, and created monumental large-scale public commissions. Among some discernible constants is an interest in the way glass permutes the interactions of mass and light, and a belief that "art is a way of slowing down time." The work incorporating found objects goes further, arresting the physical response of glass to gravity in mid-movement, and providing perceptual sculptures of surpassing clarity.

Shaffer has developed a new idiom to express her creativity whether creating with glass alone or combining it with metal objects. Her 30-year career includes numerous awards, impressive commissions, important worldwide exhibitions and contributions to collections that include The Metropolitan Museum of Art in New York City and the Smithsonian Institution in Washington, D.C.

Slumped glass, metal & wood
52 x 18 x 16"

MARY SHAFFER

FLOAT BACK

Slumped glass & metal
25½ x 10 x 6"

RICHARD C SMITH

STAIRS #2

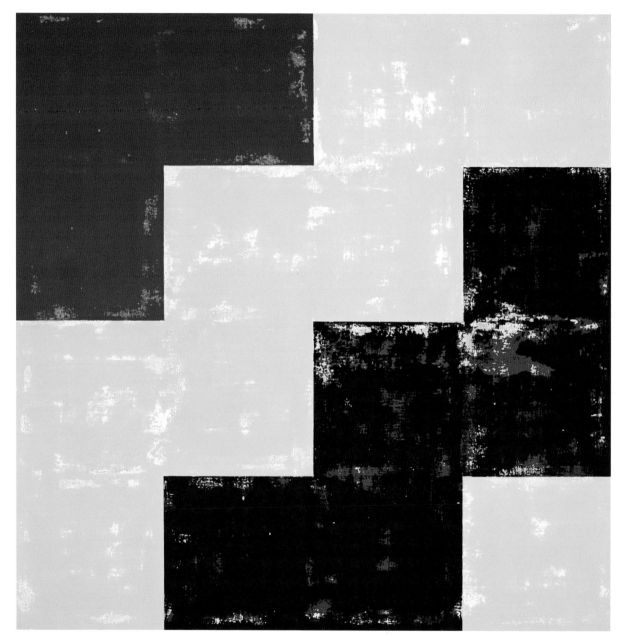

Enamel on canvas
72 x 72"

Richard C Smith is an artist who arrived in Santa Fe from his native Los Angeles. He had studied with Emerson Wolfer at Chouinard, which is now known as Cal Arts. Smith's large-scale canvases are painted with vivid primary colors that create excitement and high impact. To achieve this intensity, the artist employs a mixture of painting, photography, and various textural finishes. His use of enamel paint and waxes, plus the use of polishing equipment that is similar to automotive tools, produces a highly reflective surface that is glossy and sensuous.

Smith's work has been acquired by a variety of museums on the West Coast. He is also represented in both national and international private collections.

ALYCE FRANK

STILL LIFE WITH FLOWERS

Oil on linen
30 x 30"

Alyce Frank creates spacious compositions that let the color and energy of the New Mexico landscape shine through. A Taos resident since 1961, Frank studied with Robert Ellis, Rod Goebel and Richard Diebenkorn. She calls herself a Taos Expressionist. Her work has grown out of the Fauves, the German Expressionists and some of the classic Taos artists. Frank's works are included in many public and private collections. In 1999, New Mexico Magazine published *The Magical*

Realism of Alyce Frank, a full-length book about her work.

"My interest is in the power of the scene... to create, through color, a joyous statement about the place where I live," she says. "Art should have 'time' in it, which means that you have to break out of what you look at every day and get into something that's universal or eternal. That's why I love the landscape. It's always going to be there."

GEORGE FISCHER

BELIEVE

Oil alkyd collage
76 x 60"

George Fischer was born in 1956 in Chicago, Illinois, and has been living in the vicinity of Taos, New Mexico, since 1991. Fischer's work is a marriage of realism and abstraction, each tradition playing off the other in a balancing act of styles and influences. The ideas of the paintings are like an underlying current, making connections between the familiar and the unfamiliar. His tactile, painterly surfaces hover above strikingly realistic elements. As startling for their technical virtuosity as they are rife with complex associations, Fischer's paintings are tour-de-force works. The psychological and symbolic implications of the clothes and other items are an integral part of Fischer's work, but they are selected and arranged in a manner that is more intuitive than calculated.

George Fischer's works are included in the public collections of the Frye Art Museum, Seattle, Washington; the Philbrook Museum of Art, Tulsa, Oklahoma; the Hunter Museum of American Art, Chattanooga, Tennessee; and the New Britain Museum of American Art, New Britain, Connecticut.

WOODY GWYN

EL ALTO I

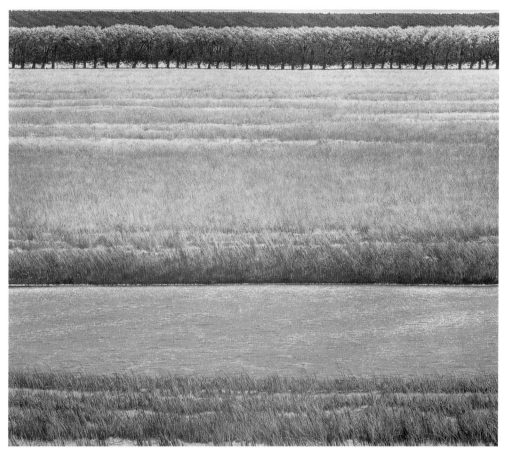

Egg tempera on canvas
72 x 84"

oody Gwyn reflects on his future plans and notes that Emerson once said, "Every cubic inch of the universe is a miracle." He muses, "Wouldn't it be wonderful to paint that way?"

M.J. Van Deventer

Gwyn, a longtime resident of New Mexico, was born in San Antonio and reared in West Texas. A realist painter, Gwyn's paintings reflect the wide horizons of his childhood.

Reflecting upon Gwyn's unique brand of realism in the monograph *Woody Gwyn*, Sharyn R. Udall states, "Woody Gwyn's painting helps us to understand that the external world is always mediated through subjective human experience. When he paints an isolated stretch of highway, a stand of trees, or, for that matter, the Grand Canyon, he opens an inquiry that involves more than earth, sky, and vegetation. His is a visual dialogue between the acute specificities of the present moment and the cumulative weight of historical vision."

Udall further acknowledges that, "these landscapes, studied slowly, invite us to consider anew the absences and presences within the land. Though tinged often with alienation, melancholy, or loss, Gwyn's subjects press quietly beyond what they describe. Like the roadcuts his brush interrogates, they slice into the western landscape with an acute visual clarity…Like the earth's surface, each mind has its own topography; Woody Gwyn's is open, fluid, expansive, like his canvases."

Gwyn's works are in numerous public, private, and corporate collections throughout the United States.

KEN O'NEIL

AT THE HEART OF IT

Mixed media on wood panel
48 x 32"

Ken O'Neil trained at the Marchutz School of Lithography, Aix-en-Provence, and the San Francisco Art Institute. He travels to the remote corners of the earth studying the teachings of elders from many cultures, often at first hand. He also investigates the symbolism and legends of individual societies. The result is a range of imagery that departs from the traditional representation of a specific place or time.

O'Neil's paintings are about the land in the old sense, a realm where the ancient stories are told and retold, and where travel occurs in the spiritual realm as well as the physical. O'Neil's observations become signposts, tiny arrows pointing to adventure on an uncharted course. These abstract works are alive with color and texture, and with tracks of a path once traveled or currently being followed. The artist attempts to bridge the worlds of science and art, and to challenge the viewer to address the contemporary issues that separate us from the richness of our past.

"For me," he says, "the sense of a finished piece is best met when a viewer can be invited into the painting and cross a boundary that he or she never crossed before. If the viewer can become aware of the process and the unanswered questions it raises, then the reward is complete."

EARL STROH

HELIOS: HOMAGE TO BURTON

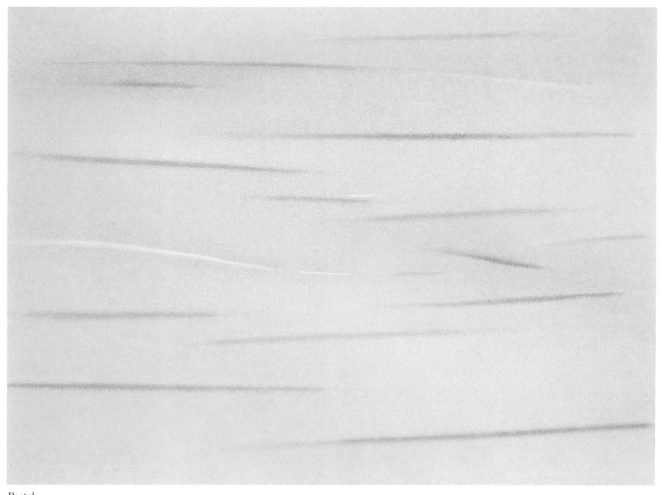

Pastel
37 x 49″

Earl Stroh was born in Buffalo, New York in 1924. In 1937 he began the serious study of art at the Art Institute of Buffalo; later, he studied under Edwin Dickinson at the Art Students League in New York City. After attending the University of New Mexico, he moved to Taos, New Mexico in 1947 and was tutored privately by Andrew Dasburg and Tom Benrimo.

In the years since, Stroh has secured his reputation as one of the most important Taos artists from the mid-twentieth century into the twenty-first. A finely tuned, immaculate abstractionist who works at a measured pace, Stroh has most recently created a radiant body of pastel and oil paintings. He produced an esteemed body of lithographs in the 1970's at the Tamarind Institute in Albuquerque, New Mexico. His etchings, primarily from the 1950's and done in Paris, are widely collected.

Stroh's work is in many museums, among which are the Art Institute of Chicago, the Cincinnati Art Museum, the Dallas Art Museum, the Fort Worth Fine Arts Museum, the University of New Mexico Art Museum, the Roswell Museum of Art, the Denver Museum of Art, the New Mexico Museum of Fine Arts, the Metropolitan Museum of Art, and the Minneapolis Art Institute. Stroh is also well represented in the private and public collections.

JOAN BOHN

ROOTS & WINGS - THE FOUR SEASONS SERIES

Winter, Spring, Summer, Autumn
Oil on wood
Each panel 42 x 15"

Joan Bohn works with ideas of construction and deconstruction, layering paint on her canvases and then going back in and removing parts to expose what is beneath. It is a process similar to the effects of weather on a wall that has been painted many times over the years. The surfaces of these elegant pieces sometimes suggest Japanese screens, or perhaps J.M.W. Turner's atmospheric skyscapes. Each viewer brings his or her own memories and sensibilities to the work, and each takes away something different. "I once was told

that my paintings could be described as 'whispers,'" says the artist, "and a whisper is far more compelling than a shout. I like that."

Time is Bohn's principal subject. She describes it as "discovering beauty through loss, and the realization that what was removed is as compelling as what remains." She is interested in the process of life itself, in the flow of thought that makes up experience. "For me," she says, "a painting must spark curiosity, engaging the mind as well as the soul."

LARRY BELL

6X6X4-AB

12MM glass coated with nickel chrome
6 x 6 x 4'
1997 Exhibition, Reykjavik Museum, Iceland

Larry Bell is one of the most noteworthy representatives of abstract art in the country. A major Los Angeles artist who has lived and worked in Taos for thirty years, he is at the height of a career that has spanned four decades and has given him an audience in all the major art centers of the world.

Bell's work has evolved in a number of directions beginning with constructions, glass boxes, and standing wall glass panel sculptures. He is best known for his "light on surface" pieces, which utilize the technology of thin deposition of vaporized metal films.

Bodies of work include *Vapor Drawings, Mirage Works,* *Furniture De Lux, Sumer,* a series of calligraphic bronze sculptures cast up to 30 feet high, and *Fractions,* a recent investigation in collage amounting to ten thousand small works on paper.

Bell exhibits extensively in museums and galleries internationally and nationally, and has been awarded numerous public art commissions. He received the New Mexico Governors Award for Excellence and Achievement in the Arts in 1990, and his work hangs in the permanent collections of the Museum of Modern Art, the Whitney Museum of American Art, and the Museum of Contemporary Art in Los Angeles, among many others.

SUZANNE DONAZETTI

ROSE INTERLUDE #2

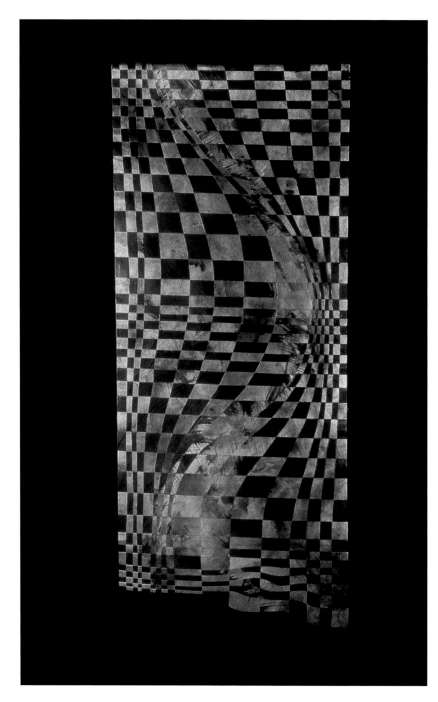

Woven copper and ink
36 x 16"

Suzanne Donazetti creates luminous, pulsating geometric abstractions on large sheets of copper, using inks, metallic acrylics, mica powders, and light-interference pigments. She starts with precise squares, circles, and triangles, then curves and spirals them into fluid motion. Her art starts out as a *tour de force* combination of structure, materials, and methods, and then evolves into a meditation on the language of color. Donazetti, who has long exhibited her work in New Mexico, strikes a universal chord in viewers with her pristine abstract work. She is a favorite of corporate collectors in Japan, New York City, and Alaska.

PASCAL

OCEAN KEY

Mahogany
48" Diameter

Pascal is a noted French sculptor who resides in Santa Fe. He has studied and exhibited in France, Italy, Monaco, and Switzerland as well as the United States. His deep knowledge of wood allows him to bring out its essential qualities in a variety of pieces, from smooth, perfect abstractions of the human form to mixed media geometrics. He pays particular attention to the selection of wood for his sculptures, and spends a great deal of time on flawless finishes that bring out the natural color. Collectors and patrons are particularly drawn to the purity of Pascal's forms, which are elegantly poised but never static. "For me," says Pascal, "wood is alive."

DICK MASON 1951-1992

TUG OF WAR

Liver spotted female tugging on knotted canvas
with black and white male
Diptych, giclée on canvas
Limited edition of 75 available
37 x 60"

Dick Mason was one of the most admired artists in Santa Fe. In his all-too-brief lifetime, he became a mature artist. His work was acquired by Amoco, Bacardi, and Trammell Crow, as well as the Oklahoma Art Center and numerous private collections. His signature Dalmatian paintings transcended the decorative to address ideas of space and repetition. Mason treated his Dalmatians as patterned form, setting them against pictures of snow-covered, piñon-dotted hillsides. The land almost, but not quite, repeated the dogs' spots, blending in with them so closely that the message of oneness was inescapable.

Mason, who readily cited the influence of Magritte and Vermeer, heightened the interplay of reality and illusion by leaving portions of the drawing visible, and by using the device of a picture within a picture. Similarly, he used windows to frame distant views when he painted the complex stonework of the ruins of Chaco Canyon.

His remarkable draftsmanship was the result of lifelong study. As a child, he drew constantly. He went on to earn a B.F.A. from the University of Iowa. His mastery of the printmaking medium was yet another example of his pursuit of perfection. Witty and paradoxical, Dick Mason's art reveals keen powers of observation and technical brilliance combined with an abiding love of life.

HILLARY RIGGS

TOUCH

Mixed media
15½ x 20″

SEEKING TRUTH

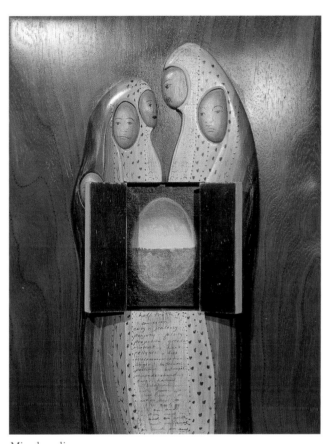

Mixed media
15½ x 20″

Hillary Riggs, the daughter of expatriate parents who ran a weaving factory in Mexico City, grew up steeped in the color, soul, and imagination of Mexican art, crafts, and culture. This experience gave her a sense of the power of art to convey concepts that are universal, yet deeply and personally felt. She earned an art degree from the University of Guanajuato and traveled to museums throughout Europe for a year of intensive independent study of art history.

Riggs moved to New Mexico twenty years ago. For much of that time she has collaborated with carvers and wood workers to create one-of-a-kind painted furniture that combines function and esthetic grace. She developed a special process for burnishing the pigments deeply into the surface in order to allow the wood grain to shine through.

She has also turned her creative eye to fine art. She is able to blend intellectual excitement, imagination, and ideas with the strong presence and visceral impact of fine craft. Her elegantly hand-carved and painted totems, wall sculptures, and paintings blend symbolism and poetry. They speak, on a collective and individual level, of the breadth of human experience. In order to stay connected with her viewers, Riggs makes a point of spending time in her gallery to visit with friends and collectors and to exchange ideas with them.

BARBARA McCAULEY

MESAS, MOUNTAINS I

"Painting is a magical act: from the emptiness of the canvas, a world comes into being. I often feel as much witness to this as creator."

Acrylic on canvas
20 x 20"

ALVARO CARDONA-HINE

THE SULTAN'S FORTRESS

"I paint what I see as if I had never seen it."

Acrylic on canvas
28 x 44"

ALVARO CARDONA-HINE

OSIRIS EMERGENT

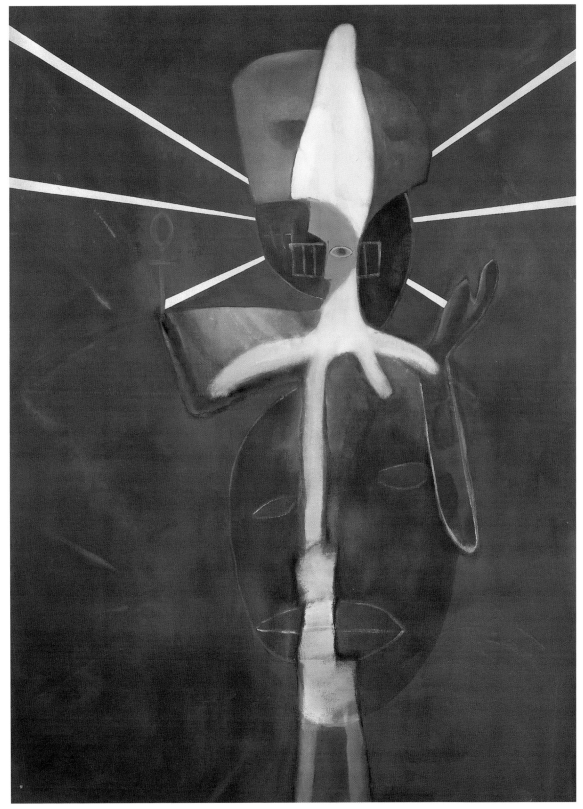

Acrylic on canvas
81 x 60"

EDWARD FLEMING

DREAM IV

Colorado Yule marble
30 x 15 x 21"

For the past twenty-five years, Edward Fleming has been an architect as well as a sculptor. He studied stone sculpture at the Corcoran School of Art in Washington, D.C., and also lived, studied, and worked in the fabled Pietrasanta, Italy. "The human form fascinates me," says Fleming. "It is holographic in that the smallest part contains the limitless beauty of the whole that, in turn, holds the wonder of the universe."

This piece is one of four that comprise a larger sculpture. When viewed together and scanned from one to the next, they work like stop-action photography, which makes the body appear to be in motion. This awakening movement is the heart of this sculpture.

GITEL RUSSO

HAWAIIAN GIRLS

Oil on canvas
78 x 68"

Gitel Russo has shown her art in many exhibitions in Europe and the United States. Her subjects are everyday vignettes raised to a level of fine art by her sensitivity to color and her intense brushwork. She allows the feeling of the moment to present itself, then lets the expression become her art.

Born in Austria and educated at the Royal Academy of Art in The Hague, Russo knew from an early age that her destiny in life was to become an artist. She has traveled widely, observing and being fascinated by people and their cultures. She considers her large oil paintings to be a reflection of the inner light of the people she meets.

JOHN AXTON

MONTEREY BAY

Oil on board
12 x 16"

J ohn Axton portrays the immense, luminous, haunting
landscape of the Southwest as few before him have
done. With the most minimal composition, he is able
to capture the sweep of the high desert and the
silence of its indigenous architecture. Working primarily
in oil, he distills the image until only the central idea
remains. Axton has a special way of describing his subject
with immaculate realism while leaving its interpretation
entirely to the viewer. He creates a meditative space on
canvas that serves as a screen for projecting all manner
of thoughts, experiences, and questions.

His work has earned accolades through the years,
including representation in the permanent collections of
the Pratt Museum in New York and the Museum of Fine
Arts in Santa Fe. Among the other museums that have
exhibited Axton's work are the Albright-Knox in Buffalo,
New York, the Philadelphia Museum, the Denver Art
Museum, the National Cowboy Hall of Fame in Oklahoma
City, and the Autry Museum of Western Heritage in Los
Angeles. In 1988, Axton was awarded an Outstanding
Alumni Achievement Award by his alma mater, Southern
Illinois University.

ROBERT T. RITTER

CHRISTO

Oil
50 x 72"

obert T. Ritter is an artist who has also been honored for his work in architecture and urban design,
as well as for interior and furniture design. As an
architect, he has led research, directorial, and advisory
boards and has enjoyed speaking engagements throughout
the United States and in Italy, Switzerland and China. He
was a professor of architecture at Texas Tech University
from 1984 to 1988.

Ritter's studio paintings are as provocative and diverse
as the multi-talented artist behind them. He renders historic
and present-day figurative subjects with a masterful hand.

The rich vibrancy of color and light in his paintings
reflects an intimate, emotional observation of the world
around him. Possessed of a marvelous, driving energy,
Ritter wields an iron grip on life, squeezing the best out
of every day, every project.

Ritter is a native Texan who lives in Santa Fe. His
best-known public artwork is a forty-foot floor mural for
the rotunda of the Texas State History Museum in Austin.
This splendid piece welcomes the museum's visitors with
a brilliantly energized bird-eye perspective of the icons,
events, and peoples in Texas history.

RAMON KELLEY

WATER DANCE "KOI"

Oil
16 x 20"

amon Kelley has exhibited his work in Santa Fe for many years. His career began quite early, when he drew in the margins of his school books in Cheyenne, Wyoming. After four years in the U.S. Navy, he won a scholarship to the Colorado Institute of Art. For many years now, he and his family have lived in Denver, where he has built an award winning reputation as one of the finest of all Southwestern artists.

Kelley is known for his work in diverse mediums, including oil, acrylic, watercolor, charcoal, conte crayon, pastel, and sculpture. He is a member of the American Watercolor Society, Allied Artists of America, Pastel Society of America, National Academy of Western Art, Knickerbocker Artists, and Oil Painters of America, Representational. In 1986, the Pastel Society of America, New York City, elected him to the Pastel Hall of Fame.

People play an important part in Kelley's paintings. His sensitive character studies are distinguished by deep insight and rich texture. His work is included in Seattle's Frye Museum of Fine Art, Spokane's Museum of Native American Cultures, Santa Fe's New Mexico Museum of Fine Art, and the West Point Military Academy, as well as many other public and private collections.

JOHN NIETO

RELIVING PAST GLORIES

Acrylic
48 x 60"

John Nieto, an internationally celebrated painter and influential interpreter of his native Southwest, is one of the most exciting and best known contemporary artists in the United States. Selected as an official artist of the 2002 Winter Olympic Games in Salt Lake City, Utah, and also invited to be the official artist for the 30th Anniversary International Balloon Fiesta of Albuquerque, New Mexico, Nieto recently created a series of brilliant serigraphs and posters commemorating each event that will thrill a worldwide audience.

Nieto's dramatic, vibrantly colored compositions have been exhibited throughout the United States and in Europe, Asia, Latin America and Africa. His paintings hang in the permanent collections of the New Mexico Museum of Fine Arts in Santa Fe, the Marine Corps Museum in Washington, DC, the Heard Museum in Phoenix, and the National Museum of Wildlife Art in Jackson Hole, Wyoming. The artist lists as the important highlights of his career, "exhibiting my work at the Grand Palais in Paris in 1983, being invited to the Oval Office by Ronald Reagan, and having a one-man retrospective show in Tokyo in 1989." It is arguable that no other single artist has ever more eloquently epitomized the spirit of the Southwest.

JEAN RICHARDSON

MIDNIGHT THUNDER

Acrylic on canvas
50 x 60"

Jean Richardson sets bands of unbridled horses racing across her canvases in spaces that suggest windswept prairie landscapes. Strokes of brilliant white seem to ignite like sparks against dark, glowing grounds. Richardson carefully balances abstract areas with recognizable forms, yet at times the representational image almost dissolves in her glorious, painterly brushwork. Richardson has exhibited her paintings in Santa Fe since the early 1980s, and has twice been featured on the cover of The Santa Fean. Her family ties in New Mexico have provided a strong connection with the culture and the landscape throughout her painting career. She has become well known for her special blend of abstraction with the imagery of the horse, a technique that emphasizes her underlying theme of spirit, motion, and energy.

ALBERT HANDELL

ABIQUIU SUNSET

Oil
22 x 28"

lbert Handell moved to Santa Fe from his native New York in 1984 and responded immediately to the late afternoon glow that illuminates adobe walls and flowered courtyards with a thousand shades of gold. The colors of his palette exploded. Handell says of his beloved New Mexico, "I have always been enthralled by the light here. I have devoted immeasurable time and energy and painting space to these skies."

Handell attended New York's heralded Art Students League, and studied in Paris at the L'École de la Grande Chaumière and the Louvre. He is honored by inclusion in the prestigious International Pastel Hall of Fame, and his paintings hang in the permanent collections of the Art Students League in New York, the Brooklyn Museum of Art, the Syracuse Museum of Art, the Schenectady Museum of Art, the Utah Museum of Art, and the Southern Alleghenies Museum of Art in Pennsylvania.

A tireless leader of painting workshops throughout America, Handell's five books on the subject are like "bibles" for countless contemporary artists. Recent accolades include the 2000 Silver Medal Award from the Laguna Plein Air Painting Competition in California, and last year, he became the first-ever recipient of the Lifetime Achievement Award from the Pastel Society of the West Coast.

PABLO ANTONIO MILAN

TURQUOISE TRAIL DANCERS

Acrylic on canvas
60 x 48"

Pablo Antonio Milan is nationally known for his contemporary art depicting the Southwest and American Indians. His distinctive layered back-washes of color form intense variations in the landscape, against which warriors, dancers, and horsemen explode in loose but power-punched brush stokes. A professional artist for seventeen years, Milan has work in corporate and private collections throughout the United States and the world. In 1997, he was named Spanish Artist of the Year in Santa Fe. Pablo Antonio Milan is a sixth genera-tion New Mexican whose family came from Spain via Mexico.

NICARIO JIMÉNEZ

THE MASK MAKER'S WORKSHOP

Mixed media: wood, gypsum, boiled potatoes
27 x 24"

Nicario Jiménez carries on a long family tradition of Peruvian folk art. Born in the small village of Alcamenca, high in the Andes, Jiménez is considered to be the foremost creator of *retablos* of his generation. In their original form, *retablos* were small portable church altars carried by Catholic priests to the remote areas of the highlands. In this century they have become unique expressions of regional cosmology and customs. Modern *retablos* depict a dual world of Heaven and Earth, populated by local deities often in the shape of native fauna and flora including the condor and the puma, corn and potatoes. Unique among *retablo* artists, Nicario Jiménez has expanded his vision to include the contemporary political events of his homeland and international subjects ranging from the streets of New York to the beaches of California. He uses a small pointed piece of wood to shape his lovely figures which are made of a gypsum and potato compound that is brightly colored with natural pigments. He often demonstrates his traditional techniques in Santa Fe.

KEVIN SLOAN

REUNION

Acrylic on canvas
60 x 54"

Kevin Sloan's paintings are loaded with illusion and reality, the concrete and the ephemeral, the formal and the organic. A world globe is a recurring theme. There are swans, many kinds of fruit, porcelain that is sometimes broken, musical notations, painted backdrops, cactus, ruins, and other fragments of memory. "My paintings strive to momentarily release us from our modern technological environment," says the artist, "into a realm of symbolism, mythology and the poet." Sloan's work is represented in the permanent collections of Chase Manhattan, Hallmark, General Electric, and the Delta Caravelle Hotel in Saigon, Vietnam, as well as the Israel Museum in Jerusalem, the Phoenix Art Museum, the Tucson Museum of Art, the Tampa Museum of Art, and the Museum of Fine Arts, Santa Fe.

RICHARD MACDONALD

ANGELIC CRYSTAL COLUMN

Bronze
6'2" x 11 x 14¾"

Richard MacDonald is a multi-dimensional artist who works on a grand scale. Known for his passionate figurative sculpture as well as monumental sculpture, he also creates drawings and other two-dimensional works that rival those of the great masters. His work is suffused with passionate emotion conveyed by extended gestures and dynamic balance.

Born and raised in California, MacDonald was educated as a painter at the Art Center School of Design. Since 1971, he has been exploring the human form through painting, drawing, and sculpture. Working exclusively with live models in the studio, he creates art that combines the fine details of anatomy with a fluid quality that suspends the figures in time and movement. He accentuates gesture and expression in order to convey the spirit of his subjects. "Drawing, painting, sculpting – historically, each is just another facet of being creative," he says. "It's not a matter of medium – it's whatever best expresses my creative idea."

MacDonald devotes years to most of his sculpture projects, working on many compositions simultaneously. His portrayal of Rudolf Nureyev was selected as part of the exhibition commemorating 100 years of the National Sculpture Society of America in Italy. His bust of Sudanese model, Latim, was also chosen by the National Sculpture Society as part of their Annual Exhibition titled "Making Faces." For his monumental sculptures, the artist designs the whole environment, including architecture, hydraulics, lighting, and fountains. One such monument is "The Flair," a twenty-six foot bronze sculpture created by the artist for the Olympic Games in Atlanta.

MacDonald is an important voice in the cause of figurative sculpture, and he backs up his words with an extraordinary ability to express muscular power, subtle emotion, and telling detail. His work has been exhibited in galleries and museums throughout Europe, Asia, and America, and has been featured in numerous art books.

EMIL BISTTRAM 1895-1976

HOMEWARD BOUND

Oil on canvas
32¾ x 40"

Emil Bisttram is considered one of New Mexico's most progressive modernist painters. His work and teachings significantly influenced the arts in the region throughout his career. As co-founder of the Transcendental Painting Group, Bisttram and fellow artist Raymond Jonson believed art could transcend the visible world and reach a higher intellectual plane through abstract, non-objective forms.

Born on the Hungarian-Rumanian border, Bisttram moved to New York around 1907. By the time he was twenty, he had established his own freelance advertising art agency, the first in the country. In 1920, Bisttram gave up the agency and devoted his energy to fine art. Studies at the National Academy of Design, the Art Students League, and the Parsons School of Design set him on a creative path which would eventually lead him from commercial design to transcendental painting.

In 1931, he received a Guggenheim Fellowship to study in Italy for two years. Fearing Mussolini's policies, Bisttram chose Mexico instead, where he studied with Diego Rivera. Upon returning to the United States, he settled in Taos, New Mexico, where he opened the Taos School of Art (renamed the Bisttram School of Art in 1943). The school drew students from around the country until its close in 1965.

Bisttram's work brought him recognition and honors throughout the nation, including exhibitions at the Whitney, Guggenheim, and Corcoran Museums.

E. IRVING COUSE 1866-1936

THE CONJURER

Oil on canvas
35¼ x 46¼"

anger Irving Couse was born in Saginaw, Michigan. His lifelong pursuit of painting Native Americans was kindled by the beauty and tranquility of the local Chippewa and Ojibwa cultures. Couse chose a career in art at an early age, studying at the Chicago Art Institute, the National Academy of Design in New York, and the Académie Julian in Paris. While in Paris, Couse married a fellow artist whose family ranch in Washington State provided him with access to a wide variety of Indian tribes. Lyrical portraits of the Klikitat, Yakima, and Umatilla were his first attempts at truly American subjects. His historical narratives of the West brought him great acclaim at the Paris Salon exhibitions.

Finding European scenes more salable, Couse returned to a successful career in France. However,

upon the advice of fellow artists Joseph Henry Sharp and Ernest Blumenschein, Couse made his first visit to Taos in 1902. Though he maintained a winter studio in Manhattan until 1928, Taos was his inspiration and became his permanent home. As a member of the Taos Society of Artists, his paintings received tremendous national exposure and made Taos a major attraction.

Couse's paintings are represented in numerous museums and private collections including the Detroit Institute of Art, the Metropolitan Museum and the National Gallery of the Smithsonian Institution. Couse created images that were highly influential in changing the public's perception of the West. His paintings are still regarded as the most poetic renderings of a vanished time.

R.C. GORMAN

THE GATHERERS

Lithograph, ed. 100
29 x 41"

R. C. Gorman's name is indivisibly linked with Contemporary American Indian Art. Perhaps there is someone, somewhere, who has never heard of him, but that is doubtful. His solid, graceful drawings, paintings, and sculptures of Navajo women are familiar to all.

Gorman was born and raised on the Navajo Reservation in northern Arizona. His ancestors were Navajo weavers, sand painters, chanters, and jewelers. As a child he herded sheep with his grandmother and learned to watch the natural world very closely and to see the beauty all around him. Like his forbears, he drew on the walls of Canyon de Chelly. Later, he studied at the university in Mexico City, where he was particularly drawn to the work of the Mexican mural painters.

R. C. Gorman's formal education was minimal, but his gift is great. Today his work hangs in the Metropolitan, the Heard Museum, the Smithsonian, the Philbrook, and the Museum of Fine Arts in Santa Fe, in addition to many other international collections, both public and private.

R.C. GORMAN

CATALINA

Acrylic on canvas
44½ x 35"

R.C. Gorman is the most famous of all the contemporary Taos artists. He has lived in that fabled art colony and maintained his own gallery for over thirty years. His work has found its way to great museums, modest homes, and private and corporate collections worldwide. Gorman was recently presented with the International Lifetime Achievement Award at the Taos Fall Arts Festival, 2001.

JANE CHERMAYEFF

UMBRIAN FIELDS

Oil
20 x 20"

Jane Chermayeff has been painting full time since she was in her thirties. She had graduated with honors from Harvard with a B.A. in anthropology and archaeology, and had studied at the Museum of Modern Art School, Rhode Island School of Design, and the Museum of Fine Arts School in Boston. Since moving permanently to Santa Fe, she has traveled and painted in Mexico, Italy and Brazil. She has won many prizes in competitive exhibits, and her work hangs in national corporations as well as private collections in the United States, Canada, and Europe.

Working in oil, acrylic, watercolor, and oil pastel, she creates strong, brilliantly colored paintings of extreme clarity. "Coming to New Mexico has caused a radical shift in my subject matter and palette," says Chermayeff. "The excitement of space, color, light, and pattern has enlivened my pleasure in seeing and my joy in the process of painting."

BARRY MCCUAN

SUNFLOWERS AND SANTA MARIA DEGLI ANGELI

Oil on canvas
30 x 24"

Barry McCuan grew naturally into his longtime career as a native New Mexico artist. Born in the state and brought up on the eastern plains, he began painting very early. His artist father took him to museums, bought him art supplies, and sent him to the university to study art.

The influence of the early Taos artists shaped his vision, but his style is distinctly his own. Few of today's artists capture the texture of the New Mexico landscape so well. McCuan is a *plein air* painter who frequently travels to Europe but concentrates on the beauty of his own surroundings in northern New Mexico. He paints in every season. He loves the long shadows of early morning and late afternoon, which give strength to his solid compositions and his beautifully realized studies of the light on the land.

MIKKI SENKARIK

SANTA FE INTRIGUE

Oil
50 x 72"

Mikki Senkarik's colors explode across her canvas like a Santa Fe sunset over the Rio Grande. With that same broad sweep, her art for the past eight years in this charming city has captivated local and visiting collectors alike.

Senkarik walked away from being one of the most recognized names in the medical illustration field in 1989, and turned her energy to painting in oils. Since selling her first canvases for modest amounts, she has become hugely successful, with a large and enthusiastic collector base to match her acclaim.

Not all has been glorious for the forty-six year old Texan. Senkarik was born prematurely, then became a cancer survivor at nineteen. Those traumas did not compare with a shockingly abusive childhood and marriage.

Her confidence returned when she met a prominent artist who became her mentor. Following her divorce, she accompanied him to Hawaii, where he not only proposed marriage but asked if he might set up the great business partnership they enjoy today. He posed two important questions: "Would you like to spend the rest of your life traveling, living in places where people go on a week's vacation?" and "Would you let me teach you to paint?"

Senkarik said yes to both. In the past thirteen years, they have accomplished everything she said yes to, and more. Today, her paintings, called "Billboards of Happiness" by her collectors, reflect her freedom, overflowing joy, and zest for living.

MIKKI SENKARIK

ENCHANTING COURTYARD

Oil
50 x 42"

ANGUS MACPHERSON

MOON CLOUD

Acrylic on canvas
50 x 52"

ngus Macpherson's massive cloudscapes are a familiar sight to New Mexicans. Some of these spectacular displays of land, sky, and weather are serenely representational; others are almost wholly abstract. Museums and such businesses as Intel and the Journal Center in Albuquerque, as well as Mount Sinai Hospital in New York, house important Macpherson canvases.

Macpherson, an Albuquerque native, was educated at the University of New Mexico. He maintains a studio in the home he shares with his wife and children in Albuquerque. He has published numerous poems and essays on art. Macpherson likens the effects of weather on the land to the effects of paint on paper or canvas. "This is our experience," he says, "logical order and understandable pattern but also chaos and upheaval. Painting is observation of the human condition. I see patterns and I see upheaval and chaos and violent turbulence and I see strange breathtaking beauty. Those elements are everywhere, in nature and society, inside and out."

FRANK MCCULLOCH

BOSQUE: CERCA DEL AGUA

Oil on linen
42 x 52"

rank McCulloch is a painter's painter and a
New Mexico institution. A recent recipient of
the Governor's Award for Visual Art, Frank has
painted seriously since the 1950's. For nearly thirty years,
he taught art in the Albuquerque public school system,
influencing many now-established artists. He has dabbled
in pure abstraction and color field painting, but always
returned to the landscape as subject matter. Now collected
worldwide, his paintings have an abstract quality that,
coupled with the personal palette and brush techniques
developed over decades of experience, evoke perfectly
the many moods of the New Mexico landscape.

ERIC R. CARNEY

ST. FRANCIS

Eric Carney is one of those rare artists who does everything, and does it well. He holds a dual B.A. from Cornell College in studio art, business and economics, and has worked as a foundry wax supervisor, a picture framer, an art representative, and a resident artist at a cultural center. He creates sculpture in stone, bronze, and other materials, and is also a painter and photographer. He has exhibited throughout the United States and in France in museum shows, neighborhood studio tours, and everything in between. Carney has traveled and studied all over the world, and speaks several languages. He seeks to identify common themes in his art. Perhaps for that reason, his work has a universal quality. "I want to bring something new to the world, or bring something back that the world has forgotten," he says.

Bronze
3 x ¾ x ¾"
Also available in life-size

ROCKING CHAIR

Alabaster
9 x 5 x 14"

NANCY KOZIKOWSKI

CHARACTERS

Hand woven, hand dyed tapestry
33 x 30"

Nancy Kozikowski has spent the last forty years absorbing the history and developing the skills of the art of tapestry. She was attracted to weaving as a teenager, and was influenced by the likes of Jasper Johns, Frank Stella, and Georgia O'Keeffe.

Kozikowski's weavings look like paintings but have the surface tactility that only weaving can provide. Stripes, being integral to most traditional weaving, have fascinated her throughout her career and she has pondered their nature thoroughly. They appear in her work in various guises such as belts, crosses, letters or flags. Her talent and dedication to her art have placed her at the forefront of a small cadre of tapestry artists whose work is finally being recognized as an art form equal to any other.

JAMES STROMBOTNE

DANCE REFLECTIONS

Acrylic on canvas
36 x 48"

J ames Strombotne's paintings radiate his unique and personal vision and commitment. They are always recognizable, whether they date from the 1960s or the 1990s, yet they show growth, change, and new experiences. They are classic in the modern sense.

Strombotne received a fellowship from Pomona College to travel in Italy, and at age twenty-seven was awarded a Guggenheim Fellowship for further study in Rome. In the years since, his work has found its way into the permanent collections of museums including the Whitney Museum of Art and the Museum of American

Art in New York, the Hirshhorn Museum in Washington, D.C., the San Francisco Museum of Art, and the Chicago Art Institute, as well as private and celebrity collections across the country. He has had over seventy solo shows and nine major retrospectives.

"I love the process of invention and discovery," says Strombotne. "My subject matter may change, but my philosophy is a constant. My goal has always been to discover and reveal, to turn the corner with each and every painting, to give form and life and beauty to the subject."

GEORGE ALEXANDER

FANTASTIC GARDEN SERIES

Ceramic
8'H

George Alexander takes clay sculpture to new dimensions because he is constantly pushing the boundaries of the medium to evolve new forms and images. His influences come from such diverse sources as Japanese and Persian textiles and Impressionist paintings, as well as primitive and tribal pottery and Italian and European ceramics. Working with contrasts and balances, Alexander fuses the glossy sophistication of European traditions with the raw and essential elements of the clay to create witty and elegant celebrations of life's vitality. The work belies its implied fragility, being crafted in a high-fire clay body, developed after years of experimentation.

Alexander's ceramic art is imbued with a sophisticated wit and humor that reflects both the integrity of its subject and the clay itself. He is called by many "the Chihuly of clay." He holds an M.F.A. and has done postgraduate work in Spain. In 1988, he moved to Santa Fe and opened a full-time studio to develop this current body of work. His art is highly prized by a continually growing body of collectors in the United States and Europe.

MELINDA K. HALL

AU BORD DE LA MER

Oil and mixed media on canvas
44 x 54"

Melinda K. Hall's singular style always puts the world a little left of center. This Santa Fe painter is well known for her red and blue dog series, her upside-down-right-side-up pitched roof houses, and many other forays into her quirky and observant take on life. Never timid with paint, Hall creates surfaces of colorful multi-layers, providing a perfect playground for her assertive visual language. This vocabulary of flattened, raw imagery forms a forceful dialectic, contrasting with the sophisticated surface work.

Hall's subject matter fuses her imagination with quotidian life, drawn from her travels (particularly France) and her animals (real or imagined). She sometimes includes subtle social commentary, ranging from the wonder and difficulty of womanhood to the dread of cocktail parties. Her humorous vision reveals a refreshing, optimistic outlook.

Since 1992, Hall's work has been displayed in numerous one-person and group shows in both gallery and museum venues. Her paintings and drawings hang in private and corporate collections worldwide.

MELINDA K. HALL

MAILLOT DE BAIN - UNE PIÈCE

Oil and mixed media on canvas
38 x 30″

DAVID PEARSON

KAMSIN

Bronze
Ed. of 9
5'10"

avid Pearson's bronze sculptures honor intangible qualities of existence through the solid rendering of female and abstract forms. Whether his works express intimate bonds between mother and child or abstracted physical incarnations of angelic beings, it is his appreciation for the innermost that is the basis of all of his work. Of late, this reverence for spirit manifests itself through a body of work depicting personal connections to the natural world. His female figures have developed a meaningful sensitivity to their environments.

The skill of this native New Mexican has been cultivated for over twenty-five years. Learning his craft at Shidoni Foundry, Pearson continued to become a leading bronze sculptor in the Santa Fe area. His sculptures have variegated textures and complex patinas, resulting in pieces that are cogent and engaging. Pearson has worked on public art projects throughout the United States. His bronzes are in corporate and private collections throughout the world.

DAVID PEARSON

NIGHTINGALE

Bronze, Ed. of 15
29"

CHARLES AZBELL

THE LIGHTS OF ENCHANTMENT

Acrylic on canvas
40 x 60"

Charles Azbell captures the essence of the high desert New Mexican skies. His use of color is dramatic, bold, and alive. Visitors to his studio sometimes mistake the paintings on the wall for windows, because the naturalistic perspective is so endlessly deep and the atmosphere so filled with brilliant light. The clouds appear to move and change colors as they float across the canvas, heightening the impression of being in the landscape itself. Azbell is a self-taught artist who has been painting for twenty-five years. He is known not only for his landscapes, but his detailed paintings of historic Pueblo pottery, inspired by his concern for the preservation of that Native American craft. As in his landscapes, the illusion is so convincing that one might lift the pots off the canvas and set them down on a table. Azbell also recreates on canvas some of the authentic tribal masks in his personal collection of African art. The timeless quality of these beautiful paintings has made them valued additions to prestigious private and corporate collections worldwide.

CHARLES AZBELL

FACE MASK OF THE DO SOCIETY – IVORY COAST

Acrylic on canvas
30 x 40"

SUZANNE BETZ

DOS CABALLITOS

Acrylic and graphite on Mylar
30 x 30"

Suzanne Betz has loved and painted horses most of her life. She finds that horses have a language of their own, which they communicate in expressive gestures. She rides every day, and spends the rest of her time painting the strong abstract and representational work for which she is so well known.

Betz builds her paintings with layer upon layer of graphite marks and brush strokes, until the essence of the subject is clearly present. Her work hangs in numerous public, private, and corporate collections, and she occasionally takes commissions for very large pieces and multi-panel screens. Betz moved to Taos from Hawaii, where she had lived and worked for years. Her work is noted for its light, depth, and subtlety of color, like the landscape of northern New Mexico.

PHIL EPP

A DISTANT VIEW

Acrylic/masonite
36 x 40"

Phil Epp was born into a Mennonite farming community on the windswept plains of Nebraska. The imprint of those isolated spaces has remained with him in his mature, uplifting images of the Western Plains and Southwest.

The crisp, confident, sculptural quality of sky and land depicted in his landscapes echo the influences of the American Regionalist painters as well as the pop art attitudes of the 1960s. These animated big sky paintings create a timeless reminder of the grandeur of our vast spaces and hint at their vulnerability through exploitation as the last frontier.

Phil Epp's paintings are in numerous museum collections throughout the Plains states and Southwest. His renderings depict a clear, open window onto the memories, mysteries and wonders of our wide open spaces.

RANCE HOOD

LAKOTA WINTER

Acrylic on canvas; giclée prints also available
40 x 50"

Rance Hood is one of the best known traditional Native American painters in the world. For over forty years, he has produced paintings that combine the legends and linear style of his Comanche ancestors with a sophisticated painting technique that incorporates abstract elements. His paintings hang in important museums and private collections. Hood has toured Germany and other areas of Europe with one-man shows, and has been included in numerous books and magazines.

Hood grew up in the home of his maternal grandparents, who taught him the old Comanche ways and val-

ues. He did not speak English until he started to school, and it might be said that his "first painting language" is still Comanche. He has been enormously successful, yet he lives and works without fanfare.

Hood's large canvas, Lakota Winter, shows four warriors riding through the snow of the northern plains. The artist's characteristic portrayal of wind and weather lends movement and life to the painting. "The winters that they may have seen long ago fall into a pattern of a Jackson Pollack painting of different streams of color," says Hood.

C.S. TARPLEY

DOUMBEQUE

Blown glass, electroformed copper and goat skin

C.S. Tarpley is internationally known for his contemporary interpretations of classic designs and motifs, executed in the medium of blown glass and precious metals. Tarpley transmutes simple materials into new and lucid visions of our collective past that call attention to our common future. Since his debut in 1996, his reputation as a creator of exquisite artifacts has increased exponentially. The American Craft Museum in Manhattan and the Rockwell Museum in Corning, New York, feature his work in their permanent collections. Tarpley has also appeared on HGTV's series "Modern Masters" and in articles and reviews published by such periodicals as Native Peoples Magazine, Southwest Arts, Urban Glass Quarterly, and The Wall Street Journal.

Tarpley groups his work into several evolving series that focus on universal motifs and world culture. His latest series, The Alhambran Drums, are fully functional glass drums with goatskin heads that produce a phenomenal sound. The shapes are based on Moroccan drums known as darabukas. In keeping with his multi-ethnic vision, Tarpley draws on the Moorish themes prevalent throughout Southern Europe and North Africa. This latest edition serves as a stunning complement to Tarpley's more well-known body of work which includes The Cibola Series, The Celtic Series, and The Zapotecs. Collectors worldwide are waiting in delighted anticipation as this extraordinary young artist's vision comes of age in the new millennium. This young American's expansive ideas and devotion to impeccability will capture the imagination of collectors for generations to come.

DENNY HASKEW

START OF THE DANCE

Bronze, ed. 21   21 x 22 x 30"

enny Haskew takes an intensely personal approach to his bronze and stone sculpture. His creative process begins and ends on an emotional note, and in between comes a blend of meditative attention to the subject and mindful observation of technique and composition. Haskew states that he tries "to enter with my eyes and my heart wide open to just see and feel the pulse of our world and what is beyond."

Always, he directs his thought toward his Native American heritage, even on the occasions when that is not his chosen theme. His Potawatomi ancestors were moved by the United States Government from the Ohio River Valley to Kansas. They relocated to Oklahoma, where they were allotted land in Potawatomi County. Haskew's dual Irish-Indian ancestry provides him with a poetic spirit and a sense of cultural history that informs each work of art. Haskew is Artist in Residence at the Inn at Loretto in Santa Fe.

COMMITTED

Bronze, ed. 7   125 x 65 x 65"

TONY JOJOLA

OUR SACRED GUARDIANS

Hand-blown glass
21 x 11 x 11"

Tony Jojola is a member of Isleta Pueblo, which is linguistically linked to Taos Pueblo. His elegant vessels refer equally to traditional Pueblo pottery shapes and the most advanced glass art being created today. Jojola is also head instructor at the Taos branch of the Hilltop Artists in Residence program from Tacoma, Washington. He was instrumental in establishing this important outpost. Lloyd Kiva New, the former I.A.I.A.

president who established a glass-blowing program at the school in the 1970s, believes the studio glass center at Taos Pueblo will evolve into one of the most significant Native American art movements since beadwork in the 1700s and metal-smithing in the 1850s. Jojola says, "There's a revolution happening on the Pueblo. What we're really starting at Taos is a national Native American glass-art movement."

JOSHUA TOBEY

DISCIPLE OF THE BEAR

Bronze, ed. 20
13 x 17 x 8"

J oshua Tobey grew up in the Santa Fe art world. From childhood on, he was surrounded by art because his father and stepmother were artists. He helped his father run ceramic molds, mount bronze on marble, and polish silver, and he listened to conversations with technicians about the quality of bronzes and patinas. He assisted his parents in delivering work and installing exhibits throughout the country. He met many famous artists, both in Santa Fe and during his travels to galleries and foundries.

Tobey was educated at Western State College in Gunnison, Colorado, where he explored the surrounding mountains and rivers. This natural beauty inspired him to become an artist in his own right. He earned a B.F.A. in sculpture, and was soon enjoying the recognition that his talent earned. He selected bronze as his primary medium because it had long been his favorite, and he chose to work in a figurative style. His subjects, which include wildlife and the relationship of people to the natural order, are solidly rooted in the Southwestern landscape. "I have always considered the outdoors my second home," says Tobey. "In nature, I feel as if I am a part of something bigger than myself."

GENE AND REBECCA TOBEY

ORION'S BELT

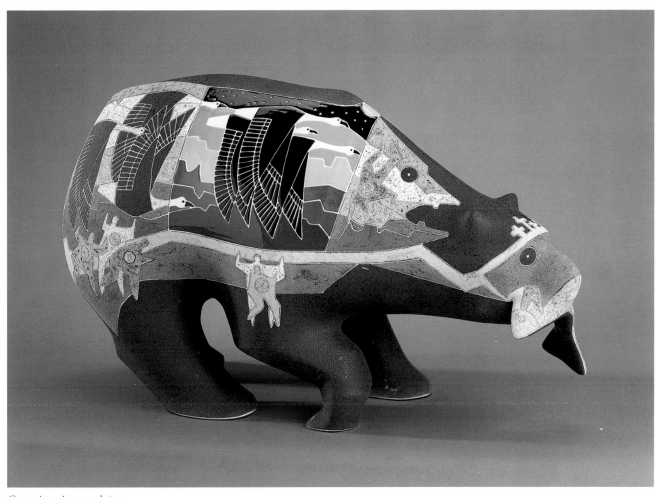

Ceramic unique sculpture
14½ x 24 x 9"

Gene and Rebecca Tobey are among the very few artists who are able to collaborate successfully on a work of art. Their process is smooth and their shared vision is seamless. Working primarily in ceramic, bronze, and watercolor, they add and subtract until each piece makes a strong statement. Representational detail is minimal, for they delve into the essence of their subjects.

Animals have always played a big part in their art and their lives. Together, they have traveled the world to see all manner of creatures in their native habitats. "Our kids call us animal charmers," they laugh. The Tobeys draw their imagery from many sources, ranging from ancient rock art and fetishes to contemporary graphics.

Beginning with a sculptural form, they apply glazes and patinas that portray landscapes, clouds, people, symbols, and geometric designs. The result is a stunningly expressive work of art.

The Tobeys each came to Santa Fe as divorced parents seeking to build a new life for their families. When they met, they blended their lives and families as well as their art. They experienced some tough times, but they persevered by means of sheer hard work. In the end, they became a powerful presence in Southwestern art. "We truly collaborate," say the Tobeys. "Each responds to the other. It isn't limiting – just the opposite. We feel we make interesting choices through the interplay of working together."

CAREY MOORE

NORTH BY NORTHWEST

Oil on canvas   40 x 30"

SPRING MELT

Oil on canvas   16 x 20"

C arey Moore arrived in Taos in 1978, after years of hoping to settle in the village she had loved and visited while working in theatre and television on both coasts. She was ready to be a visual artist. "There's a close connection between the arts," she says. "Whether it is theater or visual art, you must be aware of the dramatic moment and persuade your audience to that same awareness so they want to return for a second look."

In 1989 Moore began taking courses with the best Taos art teachers she could find. "I particularly loved painting subjects with which I had an emotional connection." Soon she was showing her work in galleries and invitationals, where her strong empathy for the area won her a devoted following. Moore is able to capture the magic and color of the place in a realistic manner, lifting it from the picturesque to the evocative.

Since those early days in Taos, she has won awards in national juried exhibitions and has had a number of one-person shows. She has served on several boards, including the Taos Institute of Art, the Visual Art Committee of the Taos Art Association, and the Harwood Foundation, where she was chair of the art committee. She is a member of Women Artists of the West. Paintings by Carey Moore are found in both private and corporate collections worldwide.

DAVE McGARY

Bronze, limited editions of Lifesize,
Masterwork, Maquette and Bust

Dave McGary, one of the most acclaimed bronze sculptors in the Southwest, is noted for his use of colored patinas that point up the intricate costumes of his Native American subjects. These magnificent life-size figures are included in many public and private collections around the world, including the Eiteljorg Museum of American Indians and Western Art. McGary, who studied in Europe with the finest bronze craftsmen in the world, has been adopted into a Native American tribe. He bases his work directly on traditional stories that he has been told by the very people he portrays.

MICHAEL HENINGTON

EL GATO CARIOCA

One member of a pride of four
Bronze
21W x 72L x 14"H

Michael Henington was born and raised on a ranch in southern New Mexico. He spent his childhood riding horses, taking care of animals, and living his dream of being a cowboy. He has led a very interesting life encompassing a variety of exciting projects that included managing rodeos and co-producing and hosting pro-rodeo television shows.

Enjoying a lifetime full of cowboy trials and tribulations brought him the opportunity to work with CNN Senior Correspondent Larry Woods shooting a documentary on small town rodeos. Three years and many performances later, Henington took his love of the West and its art to Santa Fe, where he served as director for fine art galleries. Spending most of his time with artists and collectors, Henington's ambition to develop his own artistic talent emerged and he began studying process and technique with his friend, the acclaimed sculptor, Star Liana York.

Henington created a unique style from the influences of his mentors, from Buck McCain's figurative detail to Allan Houser's modernist sculptural aesthetics. He captures the essence of his subjects' individual personalities through their irresistible expressions. Michael Henington's sculpture can be found in private and corporate collections throughout the United States and Europe.

R. BROWNELL MCGREW 1916-1994

AUBADE

Oil
35 x 45"

Brownell McGrew's work is of a quality seldom seen today. His drawings and paintings demonstrate an extraordinary connection with each of his subjects. The vitality of his sketches and the refinement of his finished works are of an intensity that bespeaks total dedication to his art. No mere academician, he has brought each canvas to a peak of lifelike realism and then has taken it a step further, making it into a work of art.

His long career began with four years of study on full scholarship at Otis Art Institute in Los Angeles. From that time on, he was a working artist whose paintings attracted a loyal group of collectors. Seeking out the most telling vistas in California's Sierras, he became known for the excellence of his landscapes.

When he moved to the Southwest, McGrew developed an affinity for the desert in all its subtle moods, and particularly for the Navajo and Pueblo Indians. The feeling was returned in full measure, for his quiet, thoughtful manner won his subjects' friendship with the man they called "Big Mac." He spent a great deal of time with them, and was privileged to record their traditional daily lives and rituals in minute detail. In addition, he spent his life refining his personal vision of the magnificent land upon which they lived.

DINAH K. WORMAN

NESTLED IN NEW MEXICO

Pastel
22 x 28"

Dinah K. Worman's landscape paintings are instantly recognizable for their clarity and depth. The thunderous distances of the Taos area are depicted with absolute fidelity. Light is everywhere. It filters through the trees and streams between the clouds. It is reflected from the walls of the adobe houses and in the water of an *acequia* flowing through a field.

Worman is able to retain this high degree of vitality because she is continually renewing her vision. "I constantly work to press beyond method and into a flow of creative instinct," she says. "One of the traps I feel an artist should avoid is becoming a mannered painter. I personally feel that mannerism is a seductive trap baited with comfort and predictability." She uses various methods of staying fresh, such as switching back and forth from oil to pastel, or intentionally mixing up her palette. This forces her to focus on the subject at hand, rather than on a habitual way of approaching the image.

Worman has earned widespread recognition for her work. She was designated a Master Pastelist by the Pastel Society of America in 1998, just four years after being elected to full membership. She has been included in invitationals throughout the West, and has had numerous solo exhibits.

She keeps her focus on the work itself, setting down her vision with a sure hand. "As a landscape artist," says Worman, "I paint the reality of my life and my time."

CHARLES MINER

TROUT SYMPHONY

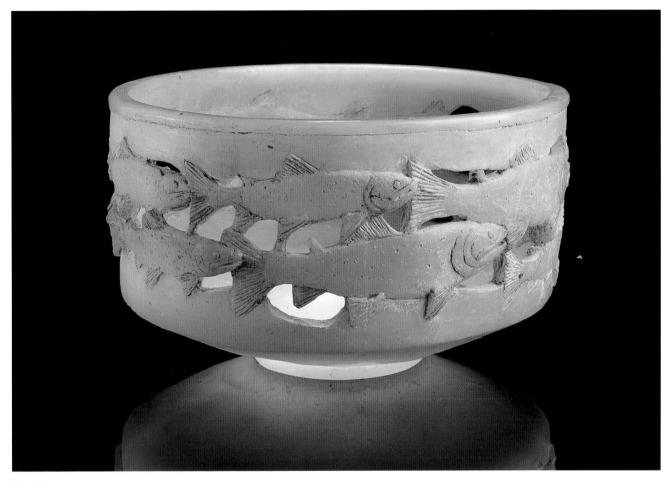

Cast glass
11 x 18"

harles Miner created classic blown glass pieces and experimented with other methods for the first half of his three-decade-long career. Then he became interested in a little used technique called Pate De Vere, which means fuse casting. His reputation soared, even as his production slowed down to accommodate the painstaking work required by this artform.

Fuse casting is basically the lost wax process that is commonly used for bronze casting. An original carving is made in wax, porcelain, or clay, and a rubber mold is cast from that. A large block of plaster with a negative mold of the art piece inside it is placed in a large electric kiln, then filled with glass that has been ground down to a fine powder. The kiln is gradually heated, as high as 1600 degrees. The glass slowly melts down into the

detailed negative imprints. This process takes fifteen to sixty days, depending on the piece. It is then gradually cooled for one to three weeks. The total production time of each 24% lead crystal piece is at least three months.

Miner built his own studio, kilns, and gallery. He works with his apprentices, assistants, and students through every phase of each process. At least one day a week he goes fly fishing, which keeps him in touch with his favorite subject matter.

Last year, Corning Glass named Charlie Miner one of the top one hundred glass artists in the world. Their museum in New York also displays one of his massive glass masterpieces.

McCreery Jordan

MARTA RIDES THE SEA

cCreery Jordan is known for her exquisitely painted, intensely lyrical art. Her style and subject matter are strictly her own, yet her constant experimentation keeps her work fresh and magical. Her mixed media pieces, in particular, reflect an astonishing ability to invoke both mystery and clarity.

Jordan, who has lived in Santa Fe for almost a decade, is an established artist who has conducted workshops throughout the United States for the past twenty years. She imparts her passion for art to her students while teaching them the solid skills that are at the heart of her own work. She is proficient in oil, acrylic, and watercolor, and she frequently combines them for maximum effect.

Jordan has published two books, and also has several videos in production. She has shown in galleries, museums, and festivals across the country, as well as an invitational exhibit in Sorrento, Italy. She has garnered many awards and other honors. Her art hangs in public venues ranging from a restaurant in France to the Wall Street Journal, as well as distinguished private collections.

Oil on linen
72 x 36"

WILLIAM BERRA

LAGO DI COMO

Oil on linen
24 x 20"

William Berra is a *plein air* painter whose light-washed scenes recall the clarity of nineteenth century European masters. Seen at a distance, Berra's figures and buildings and trees look precise and realistic, yet up close they dissolve into a kaleidoscope of brush strokes. He has a way of finding an unusual angle or the moment in time that snaps a painting to life and sets his work apart from all others.

Berra has been making art since he was a young child. In public school, he copied Old Masters and read prodigiously, then attended the Maryland Institute of Fine Arts in Baltimore. He experimented briefly with Abstract Expressionism, and found it fun but not particularly satis-

fying. He went back to traditional themes and simply taught himself his own style of painting.

During a trip through the Southwest in 1976, he arrived in Santa Fe in a blizzard and promptly left for Tucson. He returned a year later, got into a museum show in 1978, and watched his career take off. Now he exhibits extensively all over the United States, and is represented in private and public collections around the world.

He has traveled to Venice, Paris, London, and other beautiful places, but he always comes back home. He expects never to grow tired of the magnificent, ever-changing light and landscape of New Mexico.

LISA LINCH

IF YOU WERE A PEACH

Oil, acrylic & collage on canvas
42 x 40″

isa Linch is a Romantic Modernist whose work has been acquired by collectors across the country. She sets a table filled with metaphor and promise, writing her thoughts directly on the canvas and surrounding them with newspapers, tickets, stamps, and mementos from the real world. These canvases are saturated with an unsentimental nostalgia for certain cities of the heart.

As a child, Linch accompanied her father to art classes at the Chicago Art Institute and the Accademia delle Belle Arti in Florence, Italy, where she sat on the floor with her little sketchbook and worked diligently. She also developed her lifelong habit of keeping sketchbook journals. Later, the two forms merged, and art and literature became one discipline. She does not leave a painting until it has a certain rich quality. "I know it needs depth and, above all, life – motion, loose edges, sparkle, and refraction," she says. "A rhythm develops in the way I play with color, and passages lead you in and out of the canvas."

JIE-WEI ZHOU

THE LETTER

Oil
40 x 30"

ie-Wei Zhou is a master realist whose brushwork sings with a radiant Impressionistic quality. Working in oil, watercolor, and acrylic, he has won numerous awards, and has exhibited widely in China and the United States. Zhou was born in Shanghai and began studying art in middle school when his talent was recognized by his teachers. As a child, he took a sketchbook wherever he went, immersing himself in the study of light and form. Later, he earned a Masters in Fine Art. Zhou became a recognized artist in China, but he had long harbored a dream of painting and teaching in America. He sent rolled canvases to an American gallery, which sold them to pay for his passage. He is now a permanent resident of the United States.

EVELYNE BOREN

MORNING LAVENDER HARVEST, DROUIN, PROVENCE

Oil on linen
60 x 48"

E velyne Boren is one of the most internationally recognized painters in Santa Fe, as befits an artist with so cosmopolitan a background and lifestyle. She winters on the beach in Mexico and travels in Europe for several months in the spring. Every day, at home or abroad, she paints the clear, luminous, color-charged oils and watercolors for which she is famous.

Boren was born near Munich at the beginning of World War II. As a young child, she vowed that she would have a happy life when she grew up, and she proceeded to make it happen. Emigrating to America, she found work in films as an underwater stunt double, and taught herself to paint between takes. Through the years, Boren refined her technique to create the brilliant style for which she is known today.

MARILYN BENDELL

INTERMEZZO

Oil
48 x 30"

Marilyn Bendell loves the process of painting, from her first sketches to the final brush stroke. She is especially noted for her use of color and light, yet she brings a charm and subtlety to her work so that her subject shines forth. Keenly aware of the people she portrays, she is able to capture their mood on canvas. This remarkable talent has earned her many awards and honors, such as inclusion in Who's Who in American Art and Who's Who of American Women. She has been elected a Fellow of the Royal Society for the Encouragement of Arts in London.

Bendell, an American Impressionist, also is an American success story in the traditional sense. Her immense talent, combined with hard work, has carried her past adversity and kept her centered on her art, which she uses to focus on the strength and beauty of the human spirit.

MARIA MARTINEZ 1887-1980

SAN ILDEFONSO PUEBLO

San Ildefonso black plate
12"D

Maria Martinez was known primarily by her first name, Maria. She lived her entire life at San Ildefonso Pueblo, north of Santa Fe. It was she who was responsible for reviving black-on-black Pueblo pottery in the early twentieth century, and for attracting the attention of museums and collectors. Her tireless efforts not only contributed greatly to her own village, but effectively put all Indian arts and crafts on the map.

Maria occasionally made red and polychrome pots. Her hand-coiled vessels, built without a potter's wheel, were finely polished and perfectly symmetrical. The surface decoration was usually done by her husband Julian, her daughter-in-law Santana, or her son Popovi. One of the most famous Indian artists ever, she continues to inspire others through the brilliant body of work created in her lifetime.

RAPHAËLLE GOETHALS

THE IMPOSSIBILITY OF REMEMBRANCE

Encaustic on wood panel
78 x 69"

Raphaëlle Goethals, a Belgian born painter with an international reputation, creates works of powerful beauty from her studio in the foothills of the Sangre de Cristo mountains. Her meticulously rendered paintings are a result of applying layer upon layer of resin, wax, and pigment to panels of smooth birch. Skill, accident, and intuition combine to imbue her paintings with a reverence for nature, a sense of atmosphere, and a relationship to the history of skin. Writing on her work in a recent catalogue, critic Arden Reed states, "While there is nothing representational in Goethals' work, she manages to suggest something of the open spaces of northern New Mexico. Furthermore, she offers much to engage the eye. Her buildup of information encourages us to linger, to register at our leisure likeness and difference, marks of presence and of absence as they emerge and fade."

C.C. OPIELA

MERGING OF TIME

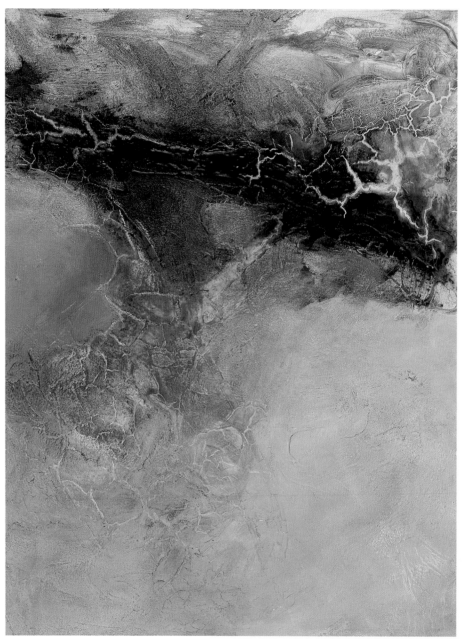

Mixed media
30 x 40"

C. Opiela is a nationally known artist who recently established a studio in Santa Fe. She lectures widely, and her list of workshops, exhibitions, honors, and public collections would fill pages. Yet, her focus is always on the work itself. She is an alchemist with a paintbrush, always finding new ideas in the expressive motion of color and texture.

At an early age, Opiela studied at the Art Institute of Chicago. She went on to study philosophy and psychology, get a university degree in studio art, and travel the Pacific, the Mediterranean, and Europe. Each experience informs the viewer of a new dimension.

Intuitive and passionate, C.C. Opiela locates the horizon of perception, the line of demarcation between sea and shore, land and sky. She finds the edge between what is seen and what is truly comprehended.

BRIGITTE BRÜGGEMANN

ICON III

Oil on linen
42 x 48"

Brigitte Brüggemann's paintings are a celebration of light, beauty, and grace. "To paint light is the challenge that makes the heart tremble," she says. Her abstract, flowerlike forms with calligraphic marks read like music, reminding the viewer to be awake, in the moment. Building layer upon layer of transparent color, she transcends technique to arrive at a language that speaks of life and its cycles.

Brüggemann, a native of Stuttgart, Germany, received her MFA in painting and drawing from the University of Colorado in Boulder. Her work is exhibited and collected nationwide as well as in Europe and Japan. Brüggemann now lives outside Santa Fe along the Pecos River. She operates a gallery that shows her own work and that of a small group of artists working with organic abstractions. The gallery space reflects her abiding sense of joy.

PAULINE ZIEGEN

LIKE A STILL PLACE

Oil and gold leaf
on wood panel
60 x 48"

Pauline Ziegen brings a modernist mind to bear on the landscape of the mythic American West. She applies today's abstraction and energetic brushwork to a rich underlying structure of classic vision and technique. Like the Old Masters and Romantic painters, she builds many layers of oil glazes to shape the light, adding 24 karat gold leaf to symbolize the richness of the earth. She etches certain lines into the surface of the underpainting before the glazing process begins, and they become an expression of time, of the movement of clouds or other things that are no longer in view.

Ziegen has always been a professional artist. She holds a B.F.A. with honors in painting and drawing from the Kansas City Art Institute. Her minimal paintings celebrate the expanse and luminosity of the land and sky in a pristine state, revealing the spiritual essence of our relationship with the land and nature. Rather than simplifying what is complex, Ziegen exposes the complex nature of true simplicity.

BLAIRE RICE BENNETT

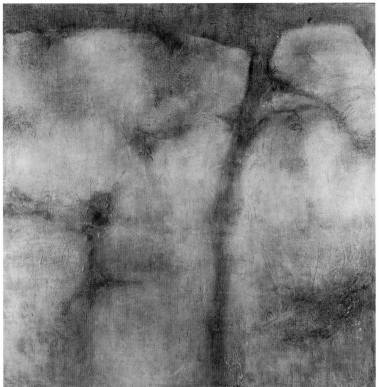

Mixed media and encaustic on wood panel
48 x 48"

Blaire Rice Bennett's thirty-five year career of art making has focused on surface and texture. Her current work is influenced by the standing stones of Scotland. The artist's careful buildup of impasto, like the encrustation of time, reveals ancient meanings and their relevance today. Each painting involves the layering, exposing, covering and uncovering of materials to make the subject visible. Bennett uses a variety of mediums, such as acrylic, oil paint, rice paper and wax to achieve this depth. The final layers are transparent glazes of encaustic, a wax heated into the surface of the painting to reveal the multitude of layers.

SALLY HEPLER

TRINITY

Hand fabricated bronze, ed. 11
23 x 24 x 17"

Sally Hepler is one of the foremost sculptors working in the field of fabricated bronze and stainless steel. Her forms are graceful and elegant; the work is executed with precision and perfection. This Santa Fe artist considers all three dimensions when creating her work, so that each angle of view becomes a unique experience. Hepler makes these sculptures from flat sheet metal that is cut, shaped, welded and finished by hand. The resulting sculptures are crisp in presentation and free in movement of form. Hepler's art speaks of beauty and sophistication. Collectors of her work include patrons from both North and South America, Europe and Asia.

JAVIER LÓPEZ BARBOSA

LLUVIA DE COLORES

Oil on canvas
60 x 50"

J avier López Barbosa makes art as naturally as he breathes, and carries his talent over into everything he does. He came to Santa Fe almost a decade ago from his birthplace of Guadalajara, Mexico. Since that time, his vivid paintings have established him as a leading abstractionist.

Barbosa is known not only for his transparent surfaces, which bring up depths of color like the heart of a jewel, but for the rich symphony of visual emotions that he uses to connect his art with those who see it.

NANCY ORTENSTONE

SONG FOR THE CHANGING SEASONS

Acrylic
60 x 48"

N ancy Ortenstone is the most readable of all abstract painters. Her audience has increased exponentially, because even those who have a lifelong allegiance to realistic work understand what she is communicating on a profoundly intuitive level. A deeply intelligent artist, she subscribes to no intellec- tualized school of art. Rather, she approaches each composition with an idea waiting to be fully realized on the canvas. Tuning each element to all the others, bringing each color up to its maximum vibration, Ortenstone connects form with dream, subject with viewer, art with life.

BRETT CHOMER

TECHOMETER

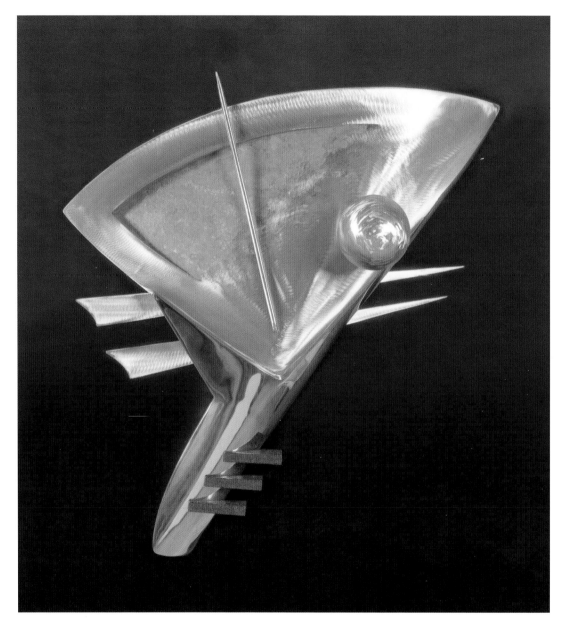

Bronze, stainless steel, granite
42 x 37"

Brett Chomer's fabricated abstract sculptures contain a wealth of cultural insight in their dynamic lines and evocative materials. He is particularly interested in the machinelike shapes of the industrial world. A longtime Santa Fe artist, Chomer has exhibited his work extensively in New Mexico and in Texas, where he received his B.F.A. from Texas Tech.

"As a kid," says Chomer, "I had the usual fascination with older cars and motorcycles. Junkyard trips provided not just parts, but a brief glimpse into a maze of history: races, accidents, owners, a million secrets. The shapes incorporated in the engines and body parts seemed to invite curiosity. I liked their repetition and the order to their assemblage. My recent pieces are minimal abstractions of larger, more complex structures. They are shapes that are prevalent in our recent social history."

BETTE RIDGEWAY

ANCIENT DANCES

Acrylic on linen
62 x 45"

Bette Ridgeway's translucent, light-filled paintings transmit a clarity of abstraction that creates a meeting place for contemplation, meditation, and dialogue. Her poured paintings quickly bring to mind the work of Morris Louis, Helen Frankenthaler, and Paul Jenkins – an influence Ridgeway freely acknowledges. Her work, however, does not reinvent but rather continues color field painting.

Ridgeway has traveled the globe, painting, teaching, and exhibiting her work while embracing the colors and customs of diverse cultures of Africa, Australia, Europe, Asia and Latin America. Moving to Santa Fe in 1996, she found the perfect environment to explore her language of light and space. Ridgeway is honored to have her work included in numerous distinguished corporate and private collections in the United States, Italy, Australia, Chile, and Japan.

GARY GROVES

UNTITLED

Giclée, ed. 5"
29 x 44½"

Gary Groves' photography captures unique moments in urban society. Primarily self taught, he is influenced by pioneering photographers such as Man Ray, Jean Tinguely, Imogen Cunningham, and others. Both his figurative and abstract works are created exclusively in 35 millimeter format and printed in strictly limited editions. Groves commands an array of processes that generate interesting juxtapositions of perception, resulting in photographs with a "hyper-real" presence. His world is at once familiar and phantasmal. Blending colorist elements with striking composition, Groves creates works that haunt the subconscious with unforgettable imagery.

THOMAS ST. THOMAS

THE REACHING SEA

Handmade paper collage on wood panel with mixed media
48 x 45"

Thomas St. Thomas has been establishing his signature in the fine art mediums of painting, sculpture, and photography, for over twenty years. St. Thomas' works, with their distinctive line drawings, impart a serene sexuality to the phenomena of the natural world. The artist has projected a viewing experience that creates existential hopefulness and spiritual ascension.

"My present creative ambitions," says St. Thomas, "have led me to believe that everything, everywhere, is art. Some of it is more poetic than others, yet each object comes with a metaphoric aura. When grouped together, the multi-symbolic structure becomes dense. By using an Everyman's alphabet, I attempt to communicate my personal life to others through the subconscious."

St. Thomas' art has been collected internationally by corporations and private institutions since he was quite young, and he has been recognized extensively throughout the United States and Mexico. The artist presently resides in Madrid, New Mexico.

BREN PRICE

CHINA LADY

Watercolor
62 x 52"

B ren Price goes beyond the appearance of her subjects and brings meaning out of process. Juxtaposing the random with the logical, she resolves the image and keeps it fresh and alive. "I believe creative expression is the pathway to human liberation," she says. "I want the viewer to become such a part of my work that he is filled with questions, not answers, that he will find something in my work that is his alone – a pathway to discovery."

A consummately professional artist, Price has taught art at all levels. She has done studies in the Americas, Europe, North Africa, China, the South Pacific, Bhutan and India. She has had numerous one-person shows. Price is the author of *Inside the Wind*, a collection of her paintings, poetry, and prose.

TERRY BALDWIN

MANDALA

Acrylic
36 x 48"

ANNIE HORKAN

ANASAZI ECHOES

Acrylic on canvas
24 x 36"

nnie Horkan is drawn to painting by the healing power of color. For twenty-six years, this prolific artist has been expressing her passion for color and her love for beauty in the creation of joyful paintings. Horkan grew up in the Virginia Piedmont in the shadow of the Blue Ridge Mountains. After many visits to New Mexico, she moved to Santa Fe in 1996. She established Bliss Studio, named after her farm in Virginia, as an art gallery and atelier where she exhibited her own work and that of local artists. Horkan has participated in numerous one-woman and group shows on the East Coast and in Paris. She is currently represented by galleries in Texas, Arizona, and Florida.

"It is color that captures me, that draws me in and speaks to me," she says. "In an instant, a simple ordinary scene or moment becomes extraordinary. It is within this blissful state that beauty blossoms, and becomes an essential ingredient to the joy and freedom of the human spirit."

Currently painting full-time in her home studio, Horkan has recently completed a series of twelve "visionary" paintings. "These new works," she explains, "combine both the inner and outer worlds into poetic visions that invite the viewer to journey more deeply into the realm of the known, and beyond, while captured by illuminating color."

DAVID DEVARY

SELF PORTRAIT IN YELLOW SLICKER

Oil and copper leaf on canvas
58 x 46"

D ave DeVary's iconic treatments of Western ranch life have the effect of deepening his characterizations of working cowboys and cowgirls. Using gold and silver leaf backgrounds, he creates a background as stark yet rich as a prairie afternoon. Raking the figures with deep shadows, he evokes the legendary quality of the American hero.

DeVary has painted seriously all his life, inspired in equal parts by great artists and Western movies. His early working years in the advertising industry won him top awards, including a handful of Clios, but he left all that behind over a decade ago to move to Santa Fe and devote all his time to his art. Since that time, his national reputation as an artist has eclipsed even his former glory.

LISA TRUJILLO

RIO GRANDE DIGEST

Hand spun churro wool
54 x 84"

Lisa Trujillo began her weaving career shortly after graduating from the University of New Mexico with a degree in marketing and an artistic bent. She married Irvin Trujillo, himself a fine weaver, and was soon learning the intricate processes of spinning and dying yarn, as well as the history of the Spanish weavers of northern New Mexico. Her designs are generally within the guidelines of traditional Rio Grande weaving, which she deeply respects although she was not born into the culture. She brings her own non-Hispanic background to her work, expressing herself in ways that create interesting and charming variations on the time-honored designs and techniques.

MARCO A. OVIEDO

AMORE II

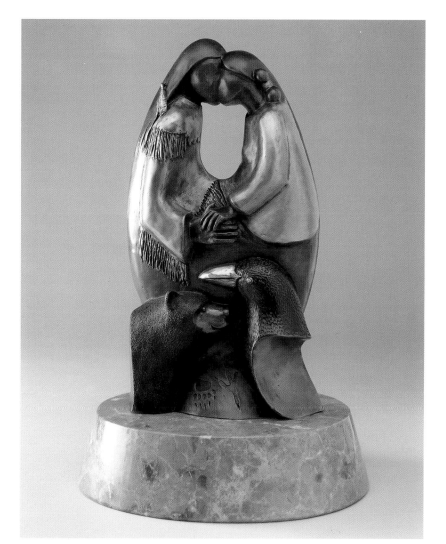

5W x 8½H x 3"D
Bronze, ltd. ed. 75

Marco A. Oviedo is a recognized woodcarver and sculptor who lives and works in the historic Chimayo Valley north of Santa Fe. As an eighth generation descendant of a family of woodworkers and woodcarvers who originated in Oviedo, the capital of the province of Asturias in Spain, he learned his wood-carving skills starting at the age of five under the careful eye of his grandfather, Aurelio Maria Oviedo. The artist's own children continue the tradition and, like their father, have works in museums and private collections.

Oviedo goes beyond tradition by creating *santos* in bronze as well as wood, and has set up a foundry to cast his sculptures using the lost wax process. Inspired by prehistoric American petroglyphs and other rock art, he interprets two-dimensional images into three-dimensional bronze sculpture. He bases his original abstract compositions on Southwestern traditions.

Marco A. Oviedo has received awards for his pieces exhibited at Spanish Market in Santa Fe, and has been featured in articles in *Sunset Magazine*, *Bon Appetit*, *National Geographic* and other periodicals. Chapters on his life and work have appeared in books on New Mexico folk art.

JOHNSTON WM. KEITH

APPEASEMENT

Oil and graphite on wood
36 x 36"

Johnston Wm. Keith creates figurative paintings with the intent of keeping the essence of drawing. In these vital images, the surface need not be covered entirely to be complete. Instead, it reveals the "back-and-forth" of decisions made by the painter. He uses the word *pentimento* to refer to this changeability of the artist's desire.

Keith traveled extensively in Europe after his formal art education. The experience provided many encounters with the religious icons that became his inspiration. He found that the awkwardness of the posture of the saints, confined in space with tilted heads and strained bodies, curiously did not look uncomfortable, but rather lost in some reverie.

In these figures, Keith brings forth an intimate sense of catching his subject in private thought. His use of color, as in his life, is sparing. He finds that if everything is tonal and he adds a bit of bright color among subdued tones, such as one red flower, the finished work sings.

ROD HUBBLE

DEEPENING TO NIGHTFALL: A TURNING POINT

Oil on linen canvas
40 x 40"
Giclée prints
32 x 32"

od Hubble has learned that art is valuable because it allows people to experience the world more clearly, to get into themselves and their awareness of nature. A friend once looked at a Hubble painting that depicted the wind moving across the grasses. Afterward, he went out and looked at the real thing and reported that he was better able to see it now. "It's about discovering life," says Hubble.

On a deeper level, he observes, "There are moments in life's journey when our challenge is greater than our everyday ability to cope – times of crisis and sadness, pain and joy. For the artist, there is but one escape. He must return to the image of beauty again and again, for within toil's depth there is solace. I am grateful to God for this transformation."

BRITT K. HAGER

CARNIVAL

Britt K. Hager is a Pacific Northwest-born artist who now lives and works in Santa Fe. She has shown her work in several West Coast cities, and has sold her work internationally. She has explored many mediums, and most recently has worked on a series of wall sculptures.

"My wall sculptures allow me to explore color, form and depth. I find my medium inspiring because it allows me to combine the qualities of painting and sculpture."

Mixed media
55 x 51 x 6"

Hager Gallery/Studio, Santa Fe

CHAS McGRATH
THE GALISTEO RIM

Pastel
14 x 30"

"I create paintings that achieve a kind of restless equilibrium with what is unspoken and unseen. Lush color is contrasted with spare composition; relationships are apparent but enigmatic and unexplained. All work toward a celebration of the phenomenal world."

CYDNEY TAYLOR

A RED & GOLDEN DAY

The power behind the paintings of Cydney Taylor has the rawness and splendor of what has been a constant celebration in the art of the last 150 years, and of its insight into the fragility of all we see. As Taylor puts it:

> "The aim is the intimate activity of expressing the particulars, a bottle or a woman or a table, the transience of their appearance and the relatedness of that appearance to the whole. I am interested in the feeling of their integration and disintegration."

Acrylic
36 x 36"

CYDNEY TAYLOR STUDIO, TAOS

SANDRA HOLZMAN
RIVER'S CREATURE

Monotype
23 x 9"

Sandra Holzman's monotypes and paintings are abstractions derived from a lifelong study of the landscape. Loading her brush with several colors at once, she applies the paint to canvas, silk, paper, or a printmaking plate. Her light touch leaves the brush stroke clearly visible, bringing the land to luminous life on the canvas.

Holzman lives in a sunlit northern New Mexico village. Her work has been shown throughout the United States and Canada, and has been featured in Architectural Digest and other major magazines. She holds a B.F.A. from the School of Visual Arts in New York City.

BENN TEDRUS FESHBACH NADELMAN

SANTA FE GARDENS, LAURA'S EYES

India ink
20 x 20"

Benn Tedrus Feshbach Nadelman is an independent artist with a universal vision. Educated at New York's renowned Art Students League and the Brooklyn Museum's art school, as well as the New Jersey Center for the Arts and The Carving Studio in Vermont, Nadelman paints in oil and watercolor, sculpts in alabaster and marble, and works in all drawing media. His award-winning paintings and drawings, vibrant mixed-media pieces, and silk-like stone carvings are represented in collections throughout the world.

"In my art," he says, "I endeavor to juxtapose Reality (Nature and Observation), Dream State (Visions and Memories) and Imagination (Creation) in order to realize a synthesis of Truth, Wisdom, Beauty, and Hope."

Nadelman has been a teaching professional, working with amateur and professional artists of all ages and skill levels, since 1988, and has lived and worked in Santa Fe since 1999. He is currently authoring a book, titled *Drawing is Seeing.*

CHARLES COLLINS

THE AMBASSADORS MEET IN WASHINGTON

Oil   64 x 68"
Bronze Figures 14"   ed. 35
Monumental Size Available

Charles Collins creates perfect Old Master canvases with Renaissance perspective and meticulous detail. The illusion is complete in every way, except that there is a delightful twist of hidden contemporary subject matter and transcendent vision that renders it universal. "My work is about the one life everywhere, how we all share the same life simultaneously," he says.

Collins' painstaking technique begins with a charcoal drawing and ends with up to thirty oil glazes. A large work can take a year to complete. The most awarded artist in the history of the Taos Art Festival, Collins has been featured on album covers for Arlo Guthrie and Michael Martin Murphey. He has been given his own day in New Mexico by the state governor, who will host Collins' exhibit at the Governor's Gallery in August 2002. "When we come together, we make something much larger than we are alone," says Collins. "We become one. All life is like petals on the same flower."

DIANA BRYER

TRES HERMANICAS

Oil on linen
36 x 36"

Diana Bryer paints world legends and the simple activities of daily life in a style that has earned widespread recognition. Her deeply intelligent yet seemingly naïve paintings are masterpieces of intricacy, disguised as simple charm. Bryer attended Chouinard Art School and the Art Center College of Design in Los Angeles, and had five one-woman shows before she was 25. She moved from California to rural northern New Mexico in 1977, and immediately became fascinated with the Hispanic and Native American cultures of the region. Her signature style incorporates elements of folk art, Jewish tradition, medieval tapestries, Indian and Persian miniatures, and Japanese woodblock prints. Her elaborately bordered compositions incorporate enough details and allegorical references to provide a lifetime of discovery. These unique pieces have been acquired by many museums as well as corporate and private collectors.

Act I Gallery 92
226D Pueblo Norte Taos, NM 87571
505.758.7831
www.actonegallery.com
actone@laplaza.org

Anderson Contemporary Cover, 30
110 W. San Francisco Santa Fe, NM 87501
Phone/Fax 505.992.0100
www.anderson-contemporary.com
director@anderson-contemporary.com

Charles Azbell Gallery 78
66 East San Francisco Street
Plaza Galeria, Suite 4 Santa Fe, NM 87501
505.988.1875
www.collectorsguide.com/azbell

Terry Baldwin Studio 113
P.O. Box 456 Truchas, NM 87578
(13ACR75)
505.689.2569/fax 505.689.2247
www.highroadnewmexico.com

Larry Bell Studio Annex 41
233 Ranchitos Road Taos, NM 87571
505.758.3062
www.larrybell.com bell@newmex.com

Marilyn Bendell Studio 99
505.455.2501
Mountain Trails Gallery
200 Old Santa Fe Trail Santa Fe, NM 87501
505.988.3444/fax 505.820.6153
mtgsantafe@aol.com

Bliss Studio 114
Post Office Box 1762 Santa Fe, NM 87504
505.954.4894 505.466.1388
888.925.4474
www.studiobliss.com
studiobliss@earthlink.net
www.collectorsguide.com/ahorkan

Brüggemann Contemporary 103
550½ Canyon Road Santa Fe, NM 87501
505.992.2553/fax 505.992.2553
www.collectorsguide.com/bruggemann

Bryans Gallery 115
121 Kit Carson Road Taos, NM 87571
505.758.9407/800.833.7631
www.bryansgallery.com mbsteger@aol.com

Diana Bryer Studio 124
313 State Road 76 on the Road to Chimayo
P.O. Box 458 Santa Cruz, NM 87567
505.753.5701/800.545.8910/fax 505.753.6578
www.dianabryer.com
dianabryer44@hotmail.com

Canyon Road Contemporary Art 106
403 Canyon Road
Santa Fe, NM 87501-2717
505.983.0433
www.collectorsguide.com/canyonrca
CRcontart@aol.com

Cardona-Hine Gallery 46
P.O. Box 326 Truchas, NM 87578
505.689.2253/fax 505.689.2903
www.onlinefineart.com
bcardona@cybermesa.com

Patricia Carlisle Fine Art 74
554 Canyon Road Santa Fe, NM 87501
505.820.0596/888.820.0596/fax 505.820.0598
www.carlislefa.com fineart@carlislefa.com

Eric R. Carney Studio 70
21 Mariano Road Santa Fe, NM 87508
505.466.1107
www.ericcarney.com ercarney@aol.com

Centinella Traditional Arts 116
HCR 64, Box 4 Chimayo, NM 87522
505.351.2180/fax 505.351.4008
877.351.2180
www.chimayoweavers.com
centinella@newmexico.com

Jane Chermayeff Studio 64
907 Canyon Road Santa Fe, NM 87501
505.989.7080
jchermayeff@aol.com

Chiaroscuro 27,58
439 Camino Del Monte Sol
Santa Fe, NM 87505
505.992.0711/fax 505.992.0387
www.chiaroscurosantafe.com
gallery@chiaroscurosantafe.com

Chimayo Trading & Mercantile 91
P.O. Box 460 Chimayo, NM 87522
505.351.4566
www.chimayoarts.com
chimayoarts@cybermesa.com

Brett Chomer Studio 108
1302½ Cerrillos Road Santa Fe, NM 87505
505.989.1155/fax 505.989.1155

Cline Fine Art 20,98
526 Canyon Road Santa Fe, NM 87501
505.982.5328/fax 982.4762
www.clinefineart.com
info@clinefineart.com

Charles Collins Gallery 123
413B Pasel Del Pueblo Norte
Taos, NM 87571
131 Los Cordovas Rt. Taos, NM 87571
505.758.2309
www.charlescollinsgallery.com
charlescollins@webtv.net

Columbine Gallery 84
211 Old Santa Fe Trail Santa Fe, NM 87501
505.988.1111/fax 505.988.1114 888.988.2778
www.columbinensg.com
columbinesantafe@att.net

Dartmouth Street Gallery 68,71
3011 Monte Vista NE
Albuquerque, NM 87106
505.266.7751 800.474.7751
www.dsg-art.com

Dearing Galleries 80,88
132 Kit Carson Road Taos, NM 87571
ph/fax 505.758.8229
www.collectorsguide.com/dearing
LDearing@taosnet.com

Deloney Newkirk Fine Art 96
634 Canyon Road Santa Fe, NM 87501
505.992.2882 800.306.9988
www.deloneynewkirk.com
info@deloneynewkirk.com

Linda Durham Contemporary Art 34,101
12 La Vega Galisteo, NM 87540
505.466.6600/fax 505.466.6699
210 Eleventh Ave. New York, NY 10001
212.337.0025/fax 212.337.0031
ldca@earthlink.net

Eldridge McCarthy Gallery 65
Sena Plaza 125 East Palace Avenue
Santa Fe, NM 87501
505.982.0380
www.eldridgemccarthy.com

Expressions in Bronze Gallery 89
2002 Sudderth Drive Ruidoso, NM 88345
505.257.3790 800.687.3424
www.expressionsinbronze.com
mcgary@zianet.com

Expressions in Fine Art 40,42
225 Canyon Road Santa Fe, NM 87501
505.988.3631/fax 505.984.2150
www.expressionsinfineart.com
inquiry@expressionsinfineart.com

Fenix Gallery 35,38
228-B North Pueblo Road Taos, NM 87571
Phone/Fax 505.758.9120
fenix@taoswebb.com
www.taoswebb.com/fenix

Andrea Fisher Fine Pottery 100
221 West San Francisco Street
Santa Fe, NM 87501
505.986.1234/fax 505.986.2002
www.andreafisherpottery.com

Edward Fleming Studio 48
#21 Avenida Vieja HC75, Box 205
Galisteo, NM 87540
505.466.2367
efa@cybermesa.com

Gallery Alexander 86
Vail, CO

Hager Gallery/Studio 120
Santa Fe, NM
505.660.3006
www.hagergallery.com
britt@hagergallery.com

Handsel Gallery 72
112 Don Gaspar Santa Fe, NM 87501
505.988.4030/800.821.1261
www.handselgallery.com

Henington Gallery 90
731 Canyon Road   Santa Fe, NM 87501
505.992.0300/fax 505.992.0303
www.heningtongallery.com

Sandra Holzman Studio 121
1612 State Road 76   Truchas, NM 87578
P.O. Box 621
Santa Fe, NM 87504
505.689.1090/fax 505.689.1080
sandrasilk@newmexico.com

Rance Hood Gallery 82
66 East San Francisco Street
Plaza Galeria, Suite 19
Santa Fe, NM 87501
903.463.6020

Rod Hubble Galleries 119
826 Canyon Road   Santa Fe, NM 87501
505.989.8077

Johnston Wm. Keith 118
551 Cordova Road #443
Santa Fe, NM 87505
505.424.8766/fax 505.424.8754
pksantafe@email.com

Kiva Fine Art 83
102 East Water Street   Santa Fe, NM 87501
505.820.7413/fax 505.820.7414
Cell: 690.3200
cstarpley@hotmail.com
www.kivaindianart.com

Margeaux Kurtie Modern Art 110
2865 State Hwy 14   Madrid, NM 87010
505.473.2250/fax 208.445.1534
www.mkmamadrid.com

Allene Lapides Gallery 29
558 Canyon Road   Santa Fe, NM 87501
505.984.0191/fax 505.982.5351
www.lapidesgallery.com

LewAllen Contemporary 93
129 West Palace Avenue
Santa Fe, NM 87501
505.988.8997/fax 505.989.8702
www.lewallenart.com
lewcontemp@aol.com

Richard MacDonald Fine Art 59
602A Canyon Road   Santa Fe, NM 87501
505.983.2482/fax 505.983.2492
866.767.8834
www.richardmacdonald.com
info@richardmacdonaldstudio.com

Manitou Galleries 97
225 Galisteo Street   Santa Fe, New Mexico
505.955.1775
www.manitougallery.com

Nedra Matteucci Galleries 60
1075 Paseo de Peralta   Santa Fe, NM 87501
505.982.4631/fax 505.984.0199
www.matteucci.com
inquiry@matteucci.com

Chas McGrath Studio 120
505.670.2808/fax 505.988.4375
cmcgrath@swcp.com

Pablo Milan Gallery 56
El Centro Shops & Galleries
102 E. Water Street   Santa Fe, NM 87501
505.982.8280/fax 505.982.8307

Minkay Andean Art 57
233 Canyon Road   Santa Fe, NM 87501
505.820.2210
dconstante@mindspring.com

Carey Moore Studio 88
P.O. Box 1893   Taos, NM 87571
505.758.9435
www.collectorsguide.com/cmoore

Mountain Trails Gallery 99
Park City, UT   435.615.8748
Weatherburn Gallery
Naples, FL   941.263.8008
Scotch Mist Gallery
Tucson, AZ   520.615.5000

**Benn Tedrus Feshbach Nadelman
Independent Arts** 122
813 Camino de Monte Rey #1
Santa Fe, NM 87505
505.310.2255
btfnfineart@yahoo.com

Navajo Gallery 63
210 Ledoux Street   Taos, NM 87571
505.758.3250
www.rcgormangallery.com
navajo@taoswebb.com

C.C. Opiela Studio 102
39 Sobradora Drive   Santa Fe, NM 87508
505.474.0904

Oviedo Carving & Bronze Gallery 117
HCR 64 Box 23A   Chimayo, NM 87522
505.351.2280/fax 505.351.2533
www.oviedoart.com
ptoviedo@cybermesa.com

Gerald Peters Gallery 32,36
1011 Paseo de Peralta   Santa Fe, NM 87501
505.954.5700/fax 505.954.5754
www.gpgallery.com

Quimera Gallery 45
206 E. Palace Avenue   Santa Fe, NM 87501
505.820.0951/fax 505.992.2837
www.quimeragallery.com
quimera@swcp.com

Bette Ridgeway Contemporary Art 109
1807 Second Street Studio 29
Santa Fe, NM 87505
505.982.0943
www.ridgewaystudio.com

Rio Grande Gallery 62
127 West Water Street   Santa Fe, NM 87501
505.983.2458/fax 505.995.0337

Karan Ruhlen Gallery 4,104
225 Canyon Road   Santa Fe, NM 87501
505.820.0807/fax 505.820.7080
www.karanruhlen.com   ruhlenart@cs.com

Gitel Russo Gallery 49
233 Canyon Road   Santa Fe, NM 87501
505.983.6782
www.gitelrusso.com

Shriver Gallery 94
401 Paseo del Pueblo Norte
Taos, NM 87571
505.758.4994/fax 505.758.8996
www.shrivergallery.com
shriver@newmex.com

Richard Smith Studio 34
3101 Old Pecos Trail #65
Santa Fe, NM 87505
505.986.9068/fax 505.989.3868
artsmith@trail.com

Alexandra Stevens Gallery of Fine Art 66
820 Canyon Road   Santa Fe, NM 87501
505.988.1311/fax 505.992.8577
115 Bent Street   Taos, NM 87571
505.758.1399/fax 505.758.7149
www.alexandrastevens.com
astevens@santafe-newmexico.com

Cydney Taylor Studio 121
243 Simpson Street   6547 NDCBU
Taos, NM 87571
505.758.0650/fax 505.758.0685
ww.cydneytaylor.com

Tobey Studios 87
P.O. Box 1685   Mason, TX 76856
915.347.5387/fax 915.347.8047
888.61TOBEY
www.tobeystudios.com   tobey@hctc.net

Gallery at Touchstone 112
110 Mabel Dodge Lane
P.O. Box 1885   Taos, NM 87571
800 or 505.758.0192/fax 505.758.3498
www.brenprice.com
www.touchstoneinn.com

Ray Tracey Gallery 87
135 W. Palace Avenue   Santa Fe, NM 87501
505.989.3430   800.336.8782
info@raytracey.com

Ventana Fine Art 50
400 Canyon Road   Santa Fe, NM 87501
505.983.8815/800.746.8815
www.ventanafineart.com

**Windsor Betts
Art Brokerage House** 44
143 Lincoln   Santa Fe, NM 87501
505.820.1234/fax 505.820.0434
www.windsorbetts.com
artinfo@windsorbetts.com

Valdez Abeyta y Valdez 31	**Jane Chermayeff** 64	**Sally Hepler** 105
Anderson Contemporary	Jane Chermayeff Studio	Karan Ruhlen Gallery
George Alexander 73	**Brett Chomer** 108	**Richard Hogan** 7
Handsel Gallery	Brett Chomer Studio	Linda Durham Contemporary Art
Sally Anderson 30	**Charles Collins** 123	**Sandra Holzman** 121
Anderson Contemporary	Charles Collins Gallery	Sandra Holzman Studio
Seth Anderson 30	**E. Irving Couse 1866-1936** 61	**Rance Hood** 82
Anderson Contemporary	Nedra Matteucci Galleries	Rance Hood Gallery
John Axton 50	**Andrew Dasburg 1887-1979** 9	**Annie Horkan** 114
Ventana Fine Art	Harwood Museum of Art	Bliss Studio
Charles Azbell 78	**David DeVary** 115	**Rod Hubble** 119
Charles Azbell Gallery	Bryans Gallery	Rod Hubble Galleries
Terry Baldwin 113	**Suzanne Donazetti** 42	**Jim Isermann** 18
Terry Baldwin Studio	Expressions in Fine Art	SITE Santa Fe
Javier Lopez Barbosa 106	**Phil Epp** 81	**Nicario Jiménez** 57
Canyon Road Contemporary Art	Dearing Galleries	Minkay Andean Art
Bill Barrett 20	**George Fischer** 36	**Jimmy Johnson** 17
Cline Fine Art	Gerald Peters Gallery	SITE Santa Fe
Kouros Gallery		
Thomas McCormick Gallery	**Edward Fleming** 48	**Tony Jojola** 85
	Edward Fleming Studio	Columbine Gallery
Larry Bell 24,41		
Larry Bell Studio Annex	**Alyce Frank** 35	**McCreery Jordan** 94
	Fenix Gallery	Shriver Gallery
Marilyn Bendell 99	Marin-Price Gallery	
Marilyn Bendell Studio		**Johnston Wm. Keith** 118
	Gagin Fujita 16	Johnston Wm. Keith Studio
Blaire Rice Bennett 105	SITE Santa Fe	
Karan Ruhlen Gallery		**Ramon Kelley** 52
	Raphaëlle Goethals 101	Ventana Fine Art
William Berra 95	Linda Durham Contemporary Art	
Shriver Gallery		**Nancy Kozikowski** 71
	R.C. Gorman 63	Dartmouth Street Gallery
Suzanne Betz 80	Navajo Gallery	
Dearing Galleries		**Lisa Linch** 96
	R.C. Gorman 62	Deloney Newkirk Fine Art
John Bingham 23	Rio Grande Gallery	
		Janet Lippincott 4
Emil Bisttram 1895-1976 60	**Gary Groves** 110	Karan Ruhlen Gallery
Nedra Matteucci Galleries	Margeaux Kurtie Modern Art	
		Harvey Littleton 22
Joan Bohn 40	**Woody Gwyn** 37	Karan Ruhlen Gallery
Expressions in Fine Art	Gerald Peters Gallery	
		Richard MacDonald 59
Evelyne Boren 98	**Britt K. Hager** 120	Richard MacDonald Fine Art
Cline Fine Art	Hager Gallery/Studio	
		Angus Macpherson 68
Emily Brock 23	**Melinda K. Hall** 74	Dartmouth Street Gallery
	Patricia Carlisle Fine Art	
Brigitte Brüggemann 103		**Agnes Martin** 13
Brüggemann Contemporary	**Albert Handell** 55	Harwood Museum of Art
	Ventana Fine Art	
Diana Bryer 124		**Maria Martinez 1887-1980** 100
Diana Bryer Studio	**Denny Haskew** 84	Andrea Fisher Fine Pottery
	Columbine Gallery	
Alvaro Cardona-Hine 47		**Dick Mason 1951-1992** 44
Cardona-Hine Gallery	**James Havard** 29	Windsor Betts Fine Art
	Allene Lapides Gallery	
Eric R. Carney 70		**Barbara McCauley** 46
Eric R. Carney Studio	**Michael Henington** 90	Cardona-Hine Gallery
	Henington Gallery	

Barry McCuan 65
Eldridge McCarthy Gallery

Frank McCulloch 69
Dartmouth Street Gallery

Dave McGary 89
Expressions in Bronze Gallery

Chas McGrath 120
Chas McGrath Studio

R. Brownell McGrew 1916-1994 91
Chimayo Trading & Mercantile

Pablo Antonio Milan 56
Pablo Milan Gallery

Charlie Miner 93
LewAllen Contemporary

Carey Moore 88
Carey Moore Studio
Dearing Galleries

Benn T.F. Nadelman 122
Benn Nadelman Independent Arts

John Nieto 53
Ventana Fine Art

Ken O'Neil 38
Fenix Gallery

C.C. Opiela 102
C.C. Opiela Studio

Nancy Ortenstone 107
Canyon Road Contemporary Art

Marco A. Oviedo 117
Oviedo Carvings and Bronze

Pascal 43
Expressions in Fine Art

David Pearson 76
Patricia Carlisle Fine Art

Flo Perkins 22
LewAllen Contemporary

Bren Price 112
Gallery at Touchstone

Louis Ribak 1903-1979 10
Gallery at Touchstone

Jean Richardson 54
Ventana Fine Art

Bette Ridgeway 109
Bette Ridgeway Contemporary Art

Hillary Riggs 45
Quimera Gallery

Robert T. Ritter 51
Ventana Fine Art

Gitel Russo 49
Gitel Russo Gallery

Fritz Scholder 26
Chiaroscuro

Mikki Senkarik 66
Alexandra Stevens Gallery

Mary Shaffer 25,32
Gerald Peters Gallery

Kevin Sloan 58
Chiaroscuro

John Sloan 6
Nedra Matteucci Galleries

Alexis Smith 17
SITE Santa Fe

Richard C. Smith 34
Linda Durham Contemporary Art
Richard Smith Studio

Jennifer Steinkamp 17
SITE Santa Fe

Earl Stroh 11, 39
Fenix Gallery
Harwood Gallery of Art

James Strombotne 72
Handsel Gallery

Henry Summa 23

Thomas St.Thomas 111
Margeaux Kurtie Modern Art

C.S. Tarpley 83
Kiva Fine Art

Cydney Taylor 121
Cydney Taylor Studio

Joshua Tobey 86
Gallery Alexander
Joshua Tobey Studio

Gene and Rebecca Tobey 87
Ray Tracey Gallery
Tobey Studios

Lisa Trujillo 116
Centinella Traditional Arts

Dinah K. Worman 92
Act I Gallery

Jie-Wei Zhou 97
Manitou Galleries

Pauline Ziegen 104
Karan Ruhlen Gallery